First Edition, 2014
Second Edition, 2015
Third Edition, 2022

ISBN-13: 978-0-9965192-4-3

Published by: Origem Publishing

Simple Zakat Guide

Understand and Calculate Your Zakat

3rd Edition, 2022

Updated with new information on
Crypto-currencies and retirement accounts

Joe W. Bradford

Table of Contents

بسم الله الرحمن الرحيم

Introduction

Why I wrote this book

If you are reading this, then you probably know the feeling. You pick up a Zakat pamphlet at the Masjid and there is just not enough information. You go research online and you find way too much. When you ask questions, you can't seem to find the answers you need. After years of teaching Zakat in communities across the US, I decided to write this book. The famous Shafi' jurist, Ibn Jama'a, said "It is most becoming to concentrate on what its most universal in benefit and address consistent needs; let a person give consideration to those topics that have yet to be written on."[1]

We all desire to fulfill our obligation to pay Zakat. Many times, we find that we do not know enough about the intimate details of our financial lives to do so confidently. We all know that Zakat is an obligation, so why are we so confused about how to calculate it? Well, because we don't know enough about ourselves. We don't know how much we consume, what we own, how much we need (as opposed to how much we want), how much we spend, or how much we save. Calculating Zakat

---

[1] - Tadhkirat al-Sami' wal-Muta'allim, Pg. 85. Beirut: Dar al-Basha'ir.

is not just a mathematical equation. It's a process of self-realization. It a process of purification[2].

If we want to fulfill this pillar of Islam, we need to uncover a deeper meaning; life is a test, wealth is a trust, and we will all be questioned about this before our feet move on the Day of Judgment. We have to come to a realization about ourselves and our purpose on this earth. Take a minute to pull back the veil from your life and see it for what it really is: amusement, diversion, glamor, ostentation, and accumulation. It is a pleasant deception and a passing delight. This all sounds negative, but if we change the way we look at our wealth, viewing it as a goal instead of a means, then and only then can we make it a source for happiness in this life and the next.

This book is an attempt to explain what Zakat is, why it's important, and how it's calculated in the simplest terms possible without dumbing things down. The faithful professional reader wants an informative, accessible book that respects both her intelligence and time. The attempt I'm making here is not to write an exhaustive tome on the variant opinions held on Zakat.

If you're looking for all the different opinions on a topic, this is not the book. Additionally, I did not want to just

---

[2] - See page 18 for more on the meanings of Zakat and purification.

provide basic information that many times leaves off important topics.

I also include some principles of Islamic financial ethics associated with Zakat. In my book "Forty Hadith for Financial Success," I speak in more detail about financial ethics and how we can change our perceptions of wealth, spending, savings, investment, and other topics to more positive, productive ones.

This New Edition

In this 2022 edition, I've made some corrections to typos that were missed in previous editions. I've also added more information about handling retirement accounts as well as paying Zakat on Cryptocurrencies. With the development of cryptocurrency, NFTs, LP tokens, and related topics, these new asset classes pose a challenge to the faithful Muslim that wants to fulfill this pillar of Islam.

Special Thanks

Before we start, I'd like to thank God for His constant blessings, then my teachers whose patience to teach me helped me gain the knowledge necessary to write this. My first teacher, Dr. Zulfiqar Ali Shah (currently of the Fiqh Council of North America) always stressed pragmatism and practicality to me as a young man when

I first accepted Islam. I hope to have channeled that drive herein.

Of the numerous teachers with whom I studied Fiqh, I find myself specifically indebted to the following teachers: Sh. Abdullah ibn Aqeel, Sh. Abdullah Ibn Khunain, Sh. Muhammad ibn Muhammad al-Mukhtar al-Shinqiti, Dr. AbdulSalam al-Suhaimi, Dr. Abdullah al-Zahem, and Sh. Ahmad Rashed al-Ruhaili. Each of them instilled in me a love for this topic and impressed upon me its importance.

I'd like to thank my students whose questions have enriched the content of both my classes and writings, and a few groups of people here in Houston who were seeds for this book to come to light. My Memorial Tafsir Class group must be thanked. I am forever indebted to their kindness, support, and love for knowledge. Islam In Spanish, founded by Mujahid Fletcher, was the first organization to host me at the Andalusia Center to deliver a 3 day weekend seminar on Zakat in 2007. The materials prepared for that seminar eventually became the book that is before you today. Mujahid and his team at Islam In Spanish will forever share the reward from this book.

There are a number of friends who've actively contributed to this work. First is Muhammad Daoudi, whose review and formatting suggestions greatly enriched the second edition. Ammar Mirza has provided invaluable feedback over the years. My longtime friend and classmate from the Islamic University of Medina, Sh. AlKhazur Sultan of Chechnya, has not only been a sounding board for Fiqhi issues, but has provided valuable input on syntax, presentation, and issues of approach. His proficiency in Islamic law, the multitude of languages he speaks, and his constant endeavor to learn and improve always humbles me and makes me question my own efforts.

Other friends that deserve mention for their input over the years are Noyan Agha and Ibrahim Saleh for their accounting and business input; Dr. Tahir Wyatt, Dr. Jonathan A.C. Brown, and Dr. Garett Davidson for the constant encouragement to write and produce useful scholarship; Sh. Nomaan Baig and Sh. Furhan Zubairi of the Institute of Knowledge (IOK) for their kindness and reassurance to write and teach; and my dear friend and big brother Kareem AbdusSalam for his brotherhood and mentorship over the years.

A Special Note to the Readers

Lastly, I'd like to thank you, the reader. Each and every one of you who has read this book and benefited from it means so much to me. From those of you who've approached me after Jumu'ah in random cities around the country to tell me you finally understood your Zakat after reading it, to those of you who've reached out over email or phone to ask additional questions and provide corrections, it is extremely encouraging to hear your feedback and see the effectiveness of this small book.

Given the positive reactions you all have shared, I often say to myself that if I have only one knowledge-based good deed to count in my scales on the day of judgment, it might just be this one.

I ask Allah to accept the good and forgive my mistakes.

Joe Bradford

Houston, TX

In the blessed month

of Sha'baan, 2022

How this guide works

You've probably purchased this book because you've seen lectures, books and seminars that tell you a lot about Zakat concepts (the why) but you're still wondering which method to use exactly when calculating (i.e., the how).

This book is the answer to both. We'll cover enough of the "why" to not be lost and enough of the "how" to get the job done effectively.

The why:

Think about this. Before you give anyone anything, a gift or a token of your respect, you usually make sure that it's worth something, or if it's edible that it's clean and wholesome. I hink about your Zakat the same way.

If we look at our personal wealth like a pie (see the graphic above) we need to be sure that the ingredients in that pie are both good for us as well as for others.

Before making that pie, we need to know what ingredients we have, what we should or shouldn't include in our recipe. You wouldn't want to include more than necessary of one ingredient, and you certainly wouldn't want to include something life threatening or poisonous. Most importantly, after knowing what to and what not to include, you'll want to know how much to measure.

Then again why make a pie, why eat one, and why give part of it away? Being wealthy is not a sin, but it's not necessarily a virtue either; the same with being poor. We'll explore some of the meanings of wealth, why we should give back, and how that only increases our wealth and betters our communities.

The how:

To get started, we'll cover some basic terms usually used in Zakat lectures. You know, the words that sound semi-exotic, but are really important to know so that you and the rest of the people you know (especially the person you ask questions of) are on the same page when discussing the topic. We'll only go over frequently mentioned terms that have transcended language barriers to become part of the Muslim vernacular.

Before we do that, I want to draw your attention to something extremely important. At the end of each section, there will be a box with a number beside it, and the text that it is connected to will be in bold in the body of text, such as this one asking you to **Please write your name below (1)**:

Please write your name below:

1	

At the end of every section, there will be one of these boxes for you to fill out. You might write your cash on hand in it, or the name of your favorite charity. Near the end of the book, all these numbers will come together, and you'll have all the information you need in one place to be able to calculate your Zakat. All you have to do at that time is add, subtract, multiply, and maybe divide, then give away your Zakat to those individuals or charities you hold near and dear. Think of it like filling out a form with a help wizard or similar. My hope is that this guide is actually simple, not just named that way.

Part One: Introductory Principles

I – Principals of Islamic Financial Ethics

When you hoard your money
you belong to it, but when you
spend it then it belongs to you.
~ Al-Aḥnaf ibn Qays

Is it wrong to be rich?

Abu ʿUbaida b. al-Jarraḥ was a wealthy man. Abu Bakr al-Siddīq was a wealthy man. Muslim and Imam Ahmed narrate that Saʿd ibn Abi Waqqas, one of the companions of the Prophet ﷺ, was a very wealthy man.

He fell sick in Makka and was afraid to die there having already moved to Medina with his only daughter. The Prophet ﷺ visited him while he was sick. He said to him "O Messenger of God, should I bequeath all my wealth?"

The Messenger of God ﷺ replied: "No."

"Then should I give away half of it?" he asked.

"No" he was told.

He said, "Well then, a third?"

To this the Prophet ﷺ replied: "A third, but even a third is much. For you to leave your family wealthy is better than leaving them dependent and begging from people.

Everything you spend on them is a Ṣadaqa, even the morsel of food you place in your wife's mouth."[3]

Being rich is not a sin but not caring for one's family is. Not fulfilling one's obligations to his family, community, and society is sinful as well. We should all strive to care for our families the best we can. This is a Prophetic imperative, one that can only be fulfilled if we work and earn.

Is poverty a virtue?

Poverty was something that the Prophet ﷺ would consistently seek refuge from. In one Prophetic tradition he is reported to have supplicated:

> "Lord, I seek refuge in you from poverty, scarcity, and humiliation, and I seek your refuge that I wrong others or myself be wronged."

Poverty is an abject state, one where you find yourself wanting of others. You can become dissatisfied with life and sometimes be driven to sinful action. This is not to say that this doesn't happen when wealthy, but it can be more likely when impoverished and needy. As a matter of faith, we should not seek to be poor, nor chase endlessly after the riches of this life. Instead, we should look at the

---

[3] - Muslim 4296.

allure of wealth like the allure of food. Eat too little and you will be malnourished and unable to function. Eat too much and you will become sluggish and apathetic.

This is a test.

Life is a test. Numerous verses in the Quran point to our losses, earnings and even accomplishments being a test.

"O you who believe: Do not betray God and the Messenger, knowingly betraying your trusts. Know that your wealth and your progeny are a trial for you, and with God is great reward." (Quran 8:27-28)

In a Prophetic tradition, the Messenger of God ﷺ said, "This world is sweet and verdant, and God has placed you as stewards herein to see how you will act."[4] In another tradition he said, "It is not poverty that I fear for you, but wealth. For if the doors to wealth are opened for you as they were for those before you, then you will go astray as they did."[5]

What is real wealth?

If this life is a test and we are placed here to steward this world, then the wealth that we are given (or

---

[4] - Muslim 7124.
[5] - Bukhari 3158.

are not) is only a means helping us pass that test. It's like the compass or ruler we used as children: some of us used them to draw circles and lines, others would poke their friends and smack their hands.

If what we know as wealth is not really "wealth," then what is? The Prophet ﷺ answered this saying "Wealth is not the accumulation of property. Wealth is wealth of the heart, wealth of the soul."[6] Commenting on this, scholars of hadith say that one of the greatest assets a person can have is contentment.

To be satisfied with enough is a hidden treasure not many of us possess. God says in the Quran (3:97), "You will never attain piety until you spend from what you love. And anything you spend, God knows it."

---

[6] - Bukhari 6446.

II - Basic terms and concepts

> *If you could invest in a treasure*
> *that can't be stolen*
> *and never depreciates*
> *would you?*
> *Do so through charity!*
> *~ Ibn Mas'ud*

Before we get started, I'd like to take a moment to go over a few terms with you. These are common words used when speaking about Zakat. They are Arabic words that have transitioned past their linguistic meaning to embody specialized meanings specific to Zakat.

Terms

- [ ] Zakat

  From a root word with the dual meaning of growth and purity, it's the proper name for the pillar of Islam and is a means for us to purify our wealth.

- [ ] Ṣadaqa

  A general term that encompasses all forms of charitable giving, including obligatory giving like Zakat.

- [ ] Niṣāb

  Meaning a designated portion, this is the amount of money you have to have to be liable for paying

Zakat. We'll refer to this in the book as "Minimum Liable Amount (Niṣāb)"

☐ Fiṭr

This word means "breaking fast;" it's used in that sense during Ramadan. When used with Zakat as in "Zakat al-Fiṭr," "Fiṭra," or "Fiṭri," it means a specific amount of food given to the poor at the end of Ramadan as an expiation for any sins or mistakes committed while fasting.

☐ Dinār

A gold coin weighing approximately 4.245 grams used during the Prophetic era.

☐ Dirham

A silver coin used in the time of the Prophet ﷺ. It was the most prevalent currency at that time. The average Dirham weighed about 2.65 grams.

☐ Mithqāl

Whereas the Dinar was a coin, the Mithqāl was its equivalent measure of weight. There were slight differences between the Dinār and Mithqāl at first, then the Dinār was standardized and these two became synonymous.

☐ Ḥawl

Zakat Year, like a fiscal year, but dealing with when you pay your Zakat. This is a lunar year, so its 11 days shorter than the regular year. We'll deal with how to calculate for the regular calendar later.

Concepts

Here are a number of rules of thumb for you to keep in mind when reading this book. These concepts are generally applicable to the rules of Zakat:

1- Zakat is not progressive.

It's a flat rate on your savings after expenses. It's not progressive, meaning it doesn't increase as your wealth increases. While we should be charitable, the Prophet ﷺ said "Start with those you care for." If each one of us started with our immediate families, then our parents and grandparents, uncles and aunts, cousins, and other family members how many people would be left in society to care for? 2.5% of any savings we retain after that will help to cover the needs of the poor and less fortunate, those that may not have that family structure to support them. Zakat encourages social stability. We give priority to our families' and communities' security, and this allows us the permanence and strength needed to then help those out of our immediate reach.

2- Zakat is a purification of your wealth.

The word Zakat comes from the Arabic root word "Z-K-Y." It has a dual meaning: growth and purity. Think of it this way: As a plant grows, it sheds foliage. It may do this to conserve resource, free itself from excess, or as a defense against infestation. When you pay your Zakat, you may be fulfilling one or all of these functions.

- You are conserving your resources by preemptively stopping greater instances of need. Imagine if no one gave charity. People's whose needs were miniscule will only increase, becoming a larger problem for society as whole.

- You are freeing yourself from excess. To grow we have to cut back a little and allow ourselves a period of renewal.

- You are defending yourself from infestation. Each of us, even with permissible earnings, makes mistakes, wrongs others, and may do some that we generally look back on and regret. By paying Zakat, you expiate those mistakes and errors. If we never allow ourselves a moment of introspection, those negative thoughts will fester and swell to become harmful later.

Zakat allows all three of these functions to happen. By giving it, you cleanse yourself of sins committed while earning it, give back to society, and allow yourself leeway for growth.

3- You only pay on what you own and control.

Your money and property are only liable for Zakat when a few conditions are met. First, you have to own it. This is pretty obvious. If it is owned by someone else, tied up in an investment and entangled with other people's money, then you don't really "own" it yet, because your share of profit and loss has not been determined. If it was lost down a well or dropped into the ocean, you don't have control over it. The only money and property that you are expected to pay Zakat on is that which you own, have full control of, and is surplus of your needs. God says in the Quran (2:219), "They ask you what they should give, say to them: What is in excess." Lastly, you do not pay Zakat on your personal property. One Prophetic tradition states "A Muslim is not obliged to pay Zakat on his horse or his servant." In our time, what is meant by this are your personal assets: your couch, your car, your residence, etc. Personal assets are exempted from Zakat.

4- You only pay on liquid wealth you can expect to benefit from.

What I mean by "you can expect to benefit from" is that the wealth you own, control, and is in surplus of your needs has some form of expected, multiplied benefit and utility. Basically, if you invested it, it would grow and increase. When we look at the types of wealth generally liable for Zakat (currency, livestock, crop yields, etc.) we'll notice that if invested or traded, they increase. This is an important principal to remember when we speak about illiquid assets later in the book.

5- You only pay on surplus wealth held for more than one year.

For most things that you pay Zakat on, you'll only pay on them when they've been in your possession for a year or more. An entire lunar year should pass on any wealth or money that you own (that meets the conditions above obviously). This condition is mentioned in a Prophetic tradition narrated by Ibn Umar: "There is no Zakat on wealth unless a lunar year passes." This narration is supported by the wide-spread established practice of the Four Caliphs and the remaining Companions of the Prophet ﷺ (May God be please with them).

There are a few exceptions to this rule, such as payouts that you get from businesses or investments made. Since they are the same type of wealth as the capital you invested, you merely add them to your ledger as an asset and calculate accordingly. So, if you have 5k USD in your account, and during the year you get paid a dividend of 350 dollars, just total it up to 5350.00 USD. This is the simplest and least problematic method of keeping a running tally of your money that you might pay Zakat on.

Part Two: Assets, Earnings, and Expenses

III – Assets (Income, Gains, & Surplus wealth)

Prayer takes you halfway.
Fasting gets you to the door.
But charity, charity gives you
an audience with the King.
~ Umar Ibn ʿAbdulAziz

Money is important. One of the pious people of the past said, "That I die and leave wealth that God questions me about is better than me needing people." How much thought have you given to how much you have, how much you owe, and how you can best grow that wealth? Zakat is due on surplus wealth. What does that mean for you? You probably go day in and day out never really thinking about how much money you have and how much you have left. We get paid through automatic deposit and charge things to our credit and debit cards. We redeem our reward points and miles and use our gift cards. We stash some cash under our mattress and deposit some of it in the bank. There are four types of wealth we include when calculating our Zakat: Cash and Cash Equivalents, Business Inventory, Livestock, and Crop Yields.

We'll sum up what these four types mean to our modern lives in the following section.

Mattress Finance

> *What a great help*
> *money is*
> *for gaining Taqwa*
> *~ Jabir Ibn Abdullah*

For many people, the most common form of finance they know is "Mattress Finance." They keep their cash and currency tucked away under their mattress, in their closet, or at home in some safe place. When calculating Zakat, the first type of wealth that we need to take into consideration is Cash and Cash Equivalents **which includes gold, silver, and all fiat currency.** Whether dollars, rupees, riyals, or pounds, we will include them below on **Cash on Hand (2a)** when calculating Zakat. We'll deal with gold and silver in the next section. If you hold cash in numerous currencies, then when you pay your Zakat, you'll need to convert them all to a single currency for calculation purposes. Here we're going to assume that you are using U.S. dollars, and so all our calculations from here on out will be in dollars.

During the time of the Prophet Muhammad ﷺ the prevalent currency was silver coin. Gold coin was in circulation as well, but not as much. In our times, fiat currency has taken the place of gold and silver coin. Later we'll talk about how we get from the Minimum Liable

Amount (Niṣāb) in Gold or Silver to modern currency. For now, think of how much cash on hand you have in your pocket, under your mattress, or in your safe, and enter that amount in line item 2a below.

Scholars have determined that fiat currency (the prevalent form of money we use today) is treated the same as gold and silver. Any cash that you have on hand, any amounts in your **Checking Account (2b)** or your **Savings Account (2c)**, or any other account or stash of money that you have immediate, unhindered access to is liable for Zakat.

Find the cash under your mattress, in your safe or safety deposit box, in your checking and savings accounts, and add them to the form below.

Please fill in the amount below

2a - Cash on Hand	________.____
2b – Checking Account	________.____
2c – Saving Account or Other Cash	________.____
Total Cash & Cash Equivalents	________.____

Gold, Silver, and Jewelry

During the time of the Prophet ﷺ the prevalent currency was silver coin. The Arabs used a coin known as the Dirham, taken from the Greek "Drachma." The neighboring Byzantine Empire was a main supplier of minted coin at that time as there were no coin mints in Arabia. The average Dirham weighed about 3 grams (2.97 grams approximately). In a Prophetic tradition the Minimum Liable Amount (Niṣāb) was two hundred (200) silver dirhams. Multiplied by 200, the weight of our Minimum Liable Amount (Niṣāb) is around 595 grams. 595 grams is the amount chosen as Minimum Liable Amount (Niṣāb) by AAOIFI, the Accounting and Auditing Organization for Islamic Financial Institutions, an international banking and finance standards body.

If you own more than 595 grams of **Silver (2d)**, then you will need to pay Zakat on the price of that amount. If you own bullion, rounds, or bars you'll need to pay Zakat on it. If you own silver jewelry exceeding 595 grams, you'll need to pay Zakat on it. If you own multiple types (bullion, rounds, jewelry, etc.) then you'll need to weigh them all together and pay on the aggregate weight.

Note: The only precious metals that Zakat is due on are gold and silver.

To give you an example of how much 595 grams of silver is (this is only an approximation) think of 20 American Eagle Silver Dollars, or a solid bar the size of an iPhone4 but around four times the weight or two 15mm wide Cuban Link Silver necklaces and a ring.

Gold during the Prophetic era was minted in Dinar, corresponding to the Latin denarius. Prophetic tradition and scholarly consensus dictate that the Minimum Liable Amount (Niṣāb) for gold was 20 Dinar. One Dinar is approximated to weigh 4.245 grams making the Minimum Liable Amount (Niṣāb) in grams 85 grams. Again 85 grams of gold is the amount chosen as Minimum Liable Amount (Niṣāb) by AAOIFI. If you have 85 grams of **Gold (2e)** or more, you'll need to pay Zakat on it.

To visual this, think of about three (3) 1 Oz. Krugerrand Gold Bullion Coins or two and one third (2 1/3) Super Bowl rings or about six (6) to eight (8) 22 karat gold bangles that are around 2 3/16 in. (5.56 cm) in diameter.

Three (3) South African Kruggerand each weighing 1 oz.

Remember this applies to ANY gold or silver you own, including but not limited to:

- Bullion, Coins, Rounds, or Bars
- Jewelry of any type*[7]
- Silverware or Dishes

Note: It is important to note that Zakat is NOT due on any precious stones in your jewelry. When in doubt about the weight, go to your local jeweler and ask them to weigh your gold or silver.

Most gold and silver sold in the United States contains other metals, gold and silver from overseas does not. Make sure your jeweler takes this into consideration. Ask them for pure gold or silver weight.

---

[7] - See my article on this at JoeBradford.net for more detail.

Enter the amounts of Silver and Gold you own in grams below:

Please enter the total grams of silver you own:

2d – Silver in grams	_________.____

Please enter the total grams of gold you own:

2e – Gold in grams	_________.____

If you do not own stocks or other similar investments (401k, IRA, 529 or similar), skip ahead to the section on illiquid investments.

Stocks (Shares) and Investment Accounts

You may own a share in a company or as some people say: you own stock in a company. I use the words stock and share interchangeably in this book. A stock or share is a unit of ownership interest in a company. They used to issue as paper certificates, but most people nowadays never see a paper certificate and simply purchase through an online broker.

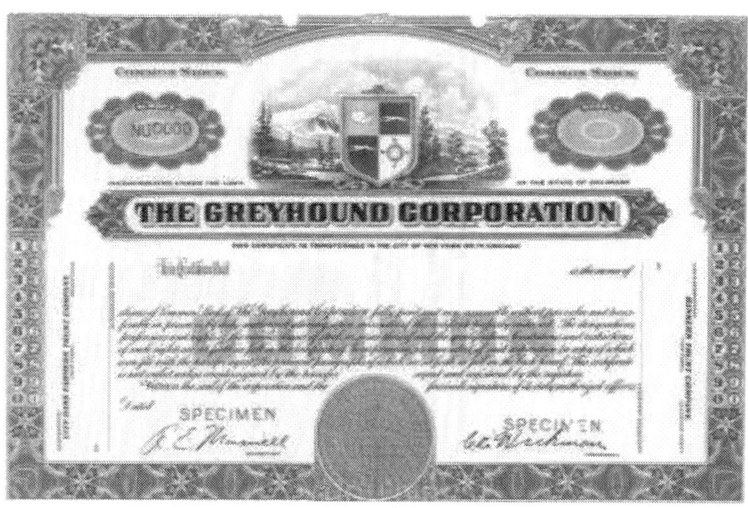

Purchasing a share does not give you control over the management of the company, but you do gain from the upside growth of that company. If the price increases, your ownership value increases in the company. If the company makes so much profit that they cannot reinvest it in the company's activities, then they will pay you a dividend.

If you own shares, you should understand how and why you own them, not just that you own them. Shares are considered liquid assets. That means that you can convert into cash quickly and that when you do the effect that will have on its price will be minimal. Consider a liquid asset to be "same as cash." Your ability to easily sell and to actively trade in these investments makes them the same as cash. Think of it like this: If these shares were cash stuffed under my mattress, would I pay Zakat on them? Yes, I would.

An example of a liquid asset is a share in Apple (APPL). You can easily sell it in the market, and you won't take any significant hit on the price. The opposite of this is an illiquid asset, one that cannot be easily converted into cash and even if it were the effect on the sell price would be sizable.

We have to ask ourselves:

- How do we own the shares we own?
- Do we own them directly or through a fund?
- Are we trading in those shares or holding them long-term?
- If we own those shares through a fund structure, how much access do we have to that fund?

We'll answer these questions and others in the following sections.

Individual Shares, Mutual Funds, ETFs, and Index Funds

If you own shares, you will either own shares of a company individually in your brokerage account or you own shares included in a Mutual Fund, ETF (Exchange Traded Fund), or similar. We'll assume that the Stock, Mutual Fund, or ETF that you own is permissible and Sharia Compliant. If the asset or company's primary earning activity is impermissible, it is obligatory to liquidate that asset and absolve yourself of any Haram earnings. For now, we'll assume that your stocks, etc. are permissible. Individual stocks are held both as passive investments for long term growth and dividends, as well as active investments for day trading, swing trading, and long and short term buy and hold strategies.

Mutual Funds

A mutual fund is a company that brings together money from many people and invests it in stocks, bonds or other assets.[8] Given this definition, it is clear that the Sharia compliance of a Mutual fund depends on what that fund holds. The stocks it holds must be permissible, it should not have bonds and fixed income instruments, and any other assets (like real estate for example) should not be leveraged assets or involved in impermissible sectors.

---

[8] - Definition per SEC website (URL: https://www.sec.gov/investor/tools/mfcc/mutual-fund-help.htm, last accessed: 3/12/22)

Mutual funds are usually held as passive investments, for long term growth and dividends.

ETFs

Exchange-traded funds (ETFs) are SEC-registered investment companies that offer investors a way to pool their money in a fund that invests in stocks, bonds, or other assets. Some ETFs are passively-managed funds that seek to achieve the same return as a particular market index (often called index funds), while others are actively managed funds that buy or sell investments consistent with a stated investment objective. ETFs are not mutual funds.[9]

Index Funds

Index funds are investment funds that follow a benchmark index, such as the S&P 500 or the Nasdaq 100. Some index funds invest in all of the companies included in an index; other index funds invest in a representative sample of the companies included in an index.[10]

---

[9] - See the SEC website for more. (URL: https://www.investor.gov/introduction-investing/investing-basics/glossary/exchange-traded-fund-etf, Last Accessed: 3/12/2022)

[10] - See for the SEC website for more. (URL: https://www.investor.gov/introduction-investing/investing-basics/glossary/index-fund, Last Accessed: 3/12/2022).

The how and why of owning shares

Now that we've defined share and the types of investments that hold publicly traded shares, when speaking about Zakat we must ask ourselves, why do I own this?

You may be actively trading in the stock market. Maybe you are a swing trader, trading over weeks and months. Maybe you are a day trader, where you are frequent buying and selling shares on the market. If this describes you, then you are an active investor. If you are buying and holding a stock waiting for the price to rise, then you are a passive investor.

Whether you buy and hold an individual stock, an ETF, or a Mutual Fund you will essentially treat them all the same for purposes of Zakat. Those holdings that are actively traded and not held for a year or more are treated as liquid investments and their total market value is used for Zakat. For stocks and funds held for more than a year or more, they are treated as passive investments, and you should follow the method defined below.

Active Investments

Active investments are constantly traded. You sit and watch the market, waiting for an upturn or downturn to take advantage of the price fluctuation. What's important are changes in price, volume, and other indicators in the market to make you money. The tool of your trade is your brokerage account. Your inventory as an active investor are the shares that you own. If this describes you, you will treat your shares the same as if you had cash in your pocket that you do business with every day. You will pay Zakat on the **Aggregate value of actively traded shares (2f).**

When including your actively traded shares in your Zakat calculations, you need to include the market value of your portfolio. If you actively trade Mutual Funds (which are basically baskets of different shares that trade at the end of the day) or ETFs (which trade intra-day), you need to include them here as well.

Please fill in the:

2f – Aggregate value of actively traded shares:	_________._____

Passive Investments

If you hold shares, mutual funds, ETFs, or index funds for longer than a year, you are not an active trader. You are a passive investor. Passive investments are the "set it and let it" type. You don't really check on them except occasionally, and rarely do you bother with them unless they generate a profit paid out to you.

You may hold an individual stock, mutual fund, or index fund long-term. You aren't actively involved in trade, nor are you interested. Your goals are two-fold, you want to preserve the value of your money invested and you want to benefit from the gains earned from the markets long-term increase.

If you are holding a stock or fund long-term, then you need to ask yourself three questions:

1- Am I holding them for 366 days or longer?
2- Am I receiving dividends?
3- When am I selling?

Question #1: Am I holding them for 366 days or longer

If you are holding them for 366 days or longer, then you will need to look to the Balance sheet[11] and identify three things:

---

[11] - You can use a site like Yahoo! Finance or Morningstar to access the balance sheet for the shares you own.

a. Cash and Cash Equivalents (C in our equation)

b. Receivables (R in our equation)

c. Inventories (I in our equation)

These three values added together are what I call the **CRI Zakat Liable Amount (2g)**. To get this amount, add the values of these three amounts together and then divide by the total number of shares issued by the company. Then, multiple that number by the number of shares that you own.

$$\left(\frac{C + R + I}{Outstanding\ Shares}\right) * \#\ of\ Shares\ Owned = CRI\ Zakat\ Liable\ Amount$$

So, let's just say that Company XYZ had 6 billion outstanding shares and you own 100 of those shares. When you go to the balance sheet, you find that the Cash and Cash Equivalents equal 15 billion, the Receivables equal 17 billion, and the Inventories are 3 billion.

$$\left(\frac{35\ billion}{6\ billion}\right) * 100\ shares = 583.34$$

In this case, the CRI Zakat Liable Amount of this long term investment is 583 dollars, which you will add to line 2g of your worksheet below.

Applying CRI values to Funds

The question that most of you have approached me about is: This is fine for individual stocks, but how do I apply this to mutual funds, ETFs, and Index Funds?

First Method: Apply it to all holdings

In calculating CRI values, you can download the holdings of each fund, calculate the CRI values for each company, pro-rate this to the weight of that company in the fund, the add all these values up to determine exactly how much of the holdings of the fund are considered liable for Zakat.

This approach is meticulous, exacting, and very tiring. Most investors do not have the time much less the skill to calculate each stock in their own portfolio, much less the hundreds of funds that are in an ETF or Mutual Fund.

Second Method: Estimate the holdings

A quicker way to find the CRI value of a stock or fund is to simply use 30% of the market value of the stock or fund. This rule of thumb is based on a survey of the market and the average CRI value of most major shares available in the market. Through my research, I've found that the average CRI value of a random stock is 25%-30%. Using this as a rule of thumb, let's take AMAGX for example, Amaanah Mutual Funds' growth fund. If the price per share of this Mutual Fund is $26.50, then 30% of that value would be $7.95. If you have 1000 shares of

AMAGX, then your total Zakat liable value for those shares would be $7950.00. 2.5% of that amount is 198.75. Compare this to paying 2.5% on the total market value, which would have been $662.50.

Why are we using the CRI amount?

Think about this. If you were a shoemaker, and you made shoes, you would not pay Zakat on your hammer, nails, and your anvil. You would pay on your pre-made shoes, standing inventory, and cash that you've made from the sale of your services. That is because those assets are liquid and easily convertible to cash, while the other assets are like the personal assets in your home or the building that you own and rent out. You pay on the liquid assets left after a year, and not the value of those assets along. Similarly with shares, you are paying on the liquid holdings and not the capital assets held by the company which generate the income and gains you are anticipating from holding them.

Please fill in the:

2g – CRI Zakat Liable Amount:	_______.____

Question #2: Am I receiving dividends?

If you receive a dividend distribution on the shares you own long term, then you need to pay on the dividend as well. Find the dividend amount issued to you per share and multiple that by the number of shares you own.

*Dividend per share * Shares Owned = Zakat Liable Dividend Amount*

If Company XYZ paid you a dividend of $0.50 per share last year and you own 100 shares, you'll add $50.00 to line below to your **Zakat Liable Dividend Amount (2h)**.

Question #3: When am I Selling?

When you decide to cash out of your long-term investments, because the shares you own represent a company and all its assets, you'll need to pay on those gains to those assets over time.

If you are selling a long-term asset, then you do not need to calculate the Zakat Liable amounts mentioned in questions #1 and #2, because they will be included in the final sales price. You will pay instead on the **Aggregate Cash out Price of long-term shares (2i)**.

Let's use an example for clarity. Say you bought shares of a company with the intention that you were going to hold them for ten (10) years.

- In year one, you owned them with the intention of it being a long term investment and you did not receive any dividends. In this case, you will pay Zakat on the CRI Value as in question #1.

- In year two, you continued to hold as a long term investor, and you also received a dividend that year. In this case, you will pay on the CRI amounts mentioned in question #1, as well as the dividends mentioned in question #2.
- In year three, you decided that you don't want to hold this stock as a long term investment anymore, and you want to sell.
  - o If you are selling during the year (but not on or near your Zakat date), then just sell the shares and add the aggregate amount you receive to your assets. When your Zakat year ends, you'll end up paying on the amounts received.
  - o If you are selling around the time, you pay your Zakat, then you don't want to double pay. How do you avoid this? By paying once on the **Aggregate Cash out Price of long-term shares (2i)**.

To get this amount, simply record the sale price of the shares you sold and pay 2.5% of the sales price. You do not need to pay on the dividends and the CRI amounts in this year, instead just pay Zakat once when you sell, because this will include the CRI amounts, the dividends, as well as any long term gains from the appreciation of the shares. If our Company XYZ sold for $50 dollars a share and you owned 100 shares, then you would $5000 to line 2i below.

Please fill in the:

2h – Zakat Liable Dividend Amount	_________._____
2i – Aggregate Cash out Price of long-term shares	_________._____

Retirement Accounts (401k, IRA, Pension Funds, etc.)

If you are working for a company, chances are that you are provided some form of benefit for retirement. In the United States, many companies will offer 401k, 457b, or similar plans to their employees. In other countries, These are called "Defined Benefits Programs." You are contributing to a set investment scheme wherein your money will be invested and reinvested over time, managed by a fund manager who will then release it to you at a later date. Both you and your employer contribute matching funds to an investment account. When you reach retirement age, all those funds and their earnings are accessible to you. You also may withdraw those funds under certain circumstances. Under some circumstances, called "Qualified Distributions" you can withdraw both contributions and gains from your account without penalty, but you will still have to pay taxes on the amounts withdrawn.[12]

Additionally, you can elect to contribute to an Independent Retirement Account (known as an IRA) that you create yourself. If you are reading this section, you probably know what a 401k, IRA, and Roth IRA is. For those that don't, a 401k is an investment fund opened through your employer. IRAs and Roth IRAs can be opened separately from an employer. They allow you to purchase from several different types of assets. Contributions to your 401k and IRA are tax deductible and qualified distributions are taxed. Contributions to a Roth IRA are taxed, but the assets in the account grow tax free and qualified distributions are not taxed.

Generally, you cannot access any of your employer's contributions until you are fully vested (you have the legal right to access those funds). The amounts that you contributed can be accessed, but only after retirement age or until a certain minimum time period is met. If you try to access these funds for any other reason other than a Qualifying Life Event[13], you will have to pay a penalty on

---

[12] - Being a first time home buyer, paying medical or education expenses, are some of the most common "Qualified Distributions." See the IRS website for a more comprehensive list of reasons for withdrawal.

[13] - Qualifying Life Events are things like a first time home purchase, educational expenses, disability or death, or medical expenses. See your financial advisor for more on what is and is not a qualifying event.

top of the taxes that you owe on these funds. If you reach retirement age or have a Qualifying Life Event After these restrictions are lifted, the asset in these accounts becomes accessible. Before your retirement age, access to these funds is restricted and there may be penalties for early withdrawal on basis, growth, or both.

The permissibility of retirement plans such as Roth IRAs and 401k plans, etc. is highly dependent on the underlying investments involved. As a general principal, all underlying investments whether they be stocks, real estate, etc. should be permissible and Sharia compliant. Assuming that the plan you are investing in is sharia compliant, how do we treat the deposits and earnings from these investment accounts? If you are not planning on making a withdrawal, there are ways to approach this.

Approach #1: Treat your 401k/IRA like cash

The first is to treat the money in these accounts as if it were cash in hand, minus the penalties you will be charged for early withdrawal and taxes (unless you are withdrawing from a Roth IRA). So, let's say you have 20k in your 401k, your tax bracket is 15%, and you have to pay a 10% penalty. Taxes will cost you 5k, your penalty will be $2,500, and the effective amount of what you would receive if you withdrew would be $18,750. You'd add this amount to **post Tax 401k distributions (2j) or post Tax**

IRA distributions (2k) and pay 2.5% on that amount, equaling $468.75.

This is the first method, even if you never withdraw the money. If you do withdraw for any reason, you still will pay Zakat on any withdrawals that you make minus taxes and penalties. We are assuming here that you are not withdrawing, and instead will leave your money in long term.

Approach #2: Treat your 401k/IRA like passive investment

If you are investing long term and have no control over the assets in your account, then you will treat the earnings from your 401k, IRA, etc. like the illiquid, passive investments mentioned previously. You will only pay Zakat on the amounts that you withdraw, i.e., **post Tax 401k distributions (2j) or post Tax IRA distributions (2k)**, which means one of two things:

- If you reach retirement age and then cash out, then you'll pay Zakat of one year only on the entire amount, then every year after (because you now have unfettered access to it.)
- If you withdraw early, then you'll pay Zakat on the net amount you withdraw after taxes and penalties.

The Approach #2 is the approach that I subscribe to and advise my clients to follow. Approach #1 above is problematic for several reasons, not the least of which is that you do not have unfettered control and access to the liquid portion of these funds without penalty. I have covered the details of these two positions elsewhere[14], but it is up to you whether you would like to pay yearly or not.

Why I prefer Approach #2

Approach #2 in summary says, "Don't pay Zakat on your 401k until you actually withdraw money or have unpenalized access to it when you retire." I prefer this approach over the first approach (paying on the full amount minus penalties and taxes) for the following reasons:

- As an investor in a long term, inaccessible investment, you are mandated by contract not to access the capital.
    - If you were to take the money out, this would be a breach of contract, which is why you are penalized.
    - The capital in this investment is therefore similar to a debt which is not in your

---

[14] - See the addendum to this book "How Zakat is paid on 401ks."

possession or an illiquid asset that you do not benefit from until you actually sell it.

- o Whether like a debt or an illiquid asset, Zakat would not be due on either until the actual funds are received, and so the 401k is treated similarly.
- Secondly, because the gains on the 401k - while they may be recognized – they are not realized.
  - o The principle of gains is that "There is no Zakat except on realized gains."[15] Therefore if gains are recognized, but not realized, they take the ruling of the capital that generated them. In this case then, there would be no Zakat on the gains as we are not paying on the capital due to its illiquidity and inaccessibility.
- Thirdly, because paying Zakat from a fund that is inaccessible would constitute a hardship. As many who are nearing retirement can tell you, that the amount of Zakat yearly can be well over their liquid wealth that they live on. While Zakat was legislated for the benefit of the poor, it was not obliged as a means to harm or setback those giving it.

---

[15] - This principle is stated by al-Qarafi, al-Nawawi, Ibn Muflih, and others.

- Lastly, one of the other prerequisites of paying Zakat is having access to the wealth in question along with the ability to spend or invest that wealth for one's own personal benefit.
  - o The scholars of the past made no differentiation between voluntary and involuntary financial choices, nor did they ever mandate that a person who entered into an agreement breach contract just to pay Zakat.

It is therefore my opinion that Zakat is not obligatory on any account you do not have full, unpenalized access to until the money is actually withdrawn or until you have full unpenalized access to.[16]

What do I do when I am ready to retire?

When retirement approaches, you may have a sizable retirement fund. It is best to prepare for the Zakat you will have to pay.

A good strategy is to pre-pay Zakat on your retirement account so that you can take full advantage of any tax credits for charitable contributions and minimize the taxes you may have to pay.

---

[16] - For more on this issue, please see my article: "Do I have to pay Zakat on my 401k?" published on my website.

It is important to consult your accountant and your financial advisor to develop a robust plan that takes this into consideration.

Please fill in the post-tax amount of 401k or IRA you cashed out on this year:

2j – post Tax 401k distributions	_________.____
2k – post Tax IRA distributions	_________.____

ESA, Coverdell & other Education Accounts

There are several types of Education Savings accounts available. Here is a list of the most common types:

- Coverdell ESA (Education Savings Account):
- 529 Account (Savings)
- 529 Account (Pre-paid)

The main differences between the first two account types listed is in the contribution limits and the withdrawal rules. Just like 401ks, IRAs, and other retirement accounts, the permissibility of education savings plans depends on the underlying investments involved. As a general principal, all underlying investments whether they be stocks, real estate, etc. should be permissible and Sharia compliant.

The third account, the pre-paid 529 account, is not an investment based account. What this means for you in the simplest terms is that you are purchasing a future place in your state's university for today's prices. Consult your financial advisor to determine if this is the right choice for you. That said, you do not pay Zakat on a pre-paid 529, because it is essentially a product/service you are purchasing for a discount, not an investment of your capital for growth.

If you've contributed to a Coverdell ESA or a 529 College Savings plan, then like your 401k or IRA we will just assume that the underlying investments are permissible. Like the 401k and IRA, you are not in control of the amounts in this account. You will treat this like passive investments or illiquid assets, IF you are using the amounts for a Qualified Higher Education Expense then you will not pay Zakat.

If you withdraw these funds for personal use or you are transferring them into your qualified IRA, then you'll treat them like your IRA and pay Zakat once on the distribution when cashing out or withdrawing. Since you must first pay a 10% fine for early withdrawal, then pay taxes on these amounts, you'll pay Zakat on the **post-tax ESA withdrawal (2l)** or the **post-tax 529 withdrawal (2m)**. Check with your financial advisor for the specific of how these fits into your tax considerations.

Please be aware that some 529 programs pay interest on a portion of the portfolio that they are invested in. If your 529 does pay interest, you will need to absolve yourself of that interest by giving it away with the intention of purifying your wealth. See the section on Haram Earnings for more info.

Please fill in the

2l – post-tax ESA withdrawals	________._____
2m – post-tax 529 withdrawals	________._____

Health FSA and HSA Accounts

A Flexible Spending Account, or FSA for short, is an account that employers prepare for their employees that allows them to deposit money tax free and use it for qualified medical expenses. The deposit limit for an FSA differs depending on whether you are using it for personal medical expenses or for your dependents as well. While FSA funds are deposited pre-tax, one of the disadvantages of the FSA is that it is owned by your employer and if you do not use the funds deposited in the FSA that year only $500 dollars can roll over to march of the next year. Any funds beyond $500 dollars left in your FSA at years end revert back to your employer. The rule for your FSA is: If you don't use it, you lose it. If you switch employers, you cannot take the funds with you.

An HSA, or Health Savings Account, is like a 401k for your health care expenses. The funds are deposited pre-tax, and you can use the funds throughout the year for qualified healthcare expenses. If you do not use them by the end of the year, they roll over to the next year and are invested. You keep both the principal and the growth in the HSA fund. If you switch employers or want to cash out the funds in your HSA or roll them over into an IRA, you can do that. The only disadvantage is that HSA accounts are limited to people with high-deductible insurance policies. Consult the documentation relevant to your find to determine the maximum amount you can deposit this year.

What about FSA accounts? Because, you never have real, unrestricted ownership over your FSA funds <u>you will not pay Zakat on any funds in the FSA account</u>. This is because you must spend this amount before the end of the year or lose the funds, therefore these funds never stay with you for an entire Zakat year.

For your HSA, because you have constant access to these funds throughout the year and they rollover to the next year when they are not spent, you will pay Zakat on the **Aggregate Amount of HSA account (2n).** Enter that amount below.

Please fill in the

2n – Aggregate Amount of HSA account	_________.____

Illiquid Assets

Illiquid means something that cannot be quickly converted to cash. Illiquid assets are those assets whose price is not readily determinable from the market. In other words, they don't have an open market with an average price; they are not fungible, and their value is only determined through negotiation and then finalized through sale.

If I own something like this, do I have to pay Zakat on it? And if I do, when do I pay it? Also, what happens if I want to sell an asset that own, but the market has taken a downturn and I can't sell?

Illiquid assets include things like:
   a) Artwork (both physical and digital).
   b) Real estate.[17]
   c) Collectibles & Antiques.
   d) Investment in privately held companies.
   e) Obsolete or "Dead" business inventory

You may be holding illiquid assets because you were unable to sell them after thinking you could. You may

---

[17] - See the section below for more details on when, what, and if you pay on Real estate.

have intentionally invested in an illiquid asset because you want to preserve the value of your money and to benefit from the gains earned from the markets long-term increase. You're only prevented from doing so by the fact that the value of what you own is not known until you sell it.

Each of these types have separate rulings. Let's discuss each of these types on its own.

Artwork (both physical and digital)

One of the objectives of Zakat is to purify the wealth of the rich by re-distributing a portion of it to the poor. If Zakat were obligated on assets that do not serve to increase the personal affluence of the person paying, we are effectively calling for a fire sale and forcing people to take a loss to fulfill a devotional obligation. This defeats the purpose and objective of Islamic law: protecting individual wealth and private property.

As far as artwork goes, it's a triple edged sword.

I)   Some people buy artwork simply as a personal asset they want to keep in their homes for aesthetic value. It doesn't matter to them if it is worth anything or not.

II)   Others are legitimate art collectors and know that certain pieces have value and will increase over time. They buy them with the purpose of arbitraging this value over the long term.

III)   Other people purposely buy illiquid assets like artwork so they can then inflate the value through appraisal, donate the artwork, and take a tax deduction.

So, if you buy artwork as a person asset, like in (I) above, you do not owe Zakat on it. If you purchase artwork like in (II) above, then Pay Zakat on the Sales Price of that artwork when you sell it - **Sales Price of Artwork you sold this year (2o)**.

If you buy artwork so that you can stash your cash and evade paying Zakat, then you must pay Zakat for each year wherein you evaded Zakat. Take the full value of the piece every year and add that to your assets. For brevity, and although you have not sold it, you still must pay Zakat on it because you're trying to evade doing so. Include the value in **Sales Price of Artwork you sold this year (2o)** below.

Please note: If you received an illiquid asset as a gift or through inheritance, then ask yourself why you are holding it, just like the situations I-III above. If you fall into situation II or III, then to be on the safe side you can add it your current account and calculate your zakat on it for the year your received it in, even though a year hasn't passed. In this case, you'd be paying early on at least a portion of it. If for some reason or another you don't want to pay Zakat on it for this year, you can hold it for one year before it becomes liable for Zakat.

Please fill in the

2o – Sales Price of Artwork you sold this year:	___________.______

Real Estate

If you own property, make sure your property falls into the right category.

- If the property your residence, then you DO NOT pay Zakat on this as mentioned previously.
- If you rent out this property, see the next section for more details.
- If this property is active on the market and up for sale, then you will pay Zakat on **Market Value of Real Estate active on the mark (2p)** (i.e., the amount you would earn if you sold it at this moment).
- If you own this property but do not have plans for it, then treat it like your passive investments and pay Zakat once on the **Value received from sale of the inactive property (2q)**.

Please fill in the

2p –Market Value of Real Estate active on the market:	_______.____
2q –Value received from sale of inactive property:	_______.____

Rentals and Lease Income

If you own properties that you rent or lease you must pay Zakat on them. You do not need to pay on the property value, only on the rental income. The short and sweet version of this here is these properties are considered personal assets, and as such are your "tools of the trade" if you will. If you were a metal worker who made steel bowls, you would sell the bowls, you wouldn't sell the machines that produced them. If your earnings from selling the steel bowls were more than the Minimum Liable Amount (Niṣāb) then you'd pay Zakat on the amount of those earnings. You wouldn't pay on the value of your hammer, anvil, and other tools. Likewise, the house, condo, or apartment you rent to others are the tools of your trade. The **Aggregate value of rental income (2r)** from these properties are the income that you will pay Zakat on.

Please fill in the

2r – Aggregate value of rental income*: * Exclude if already included with cash, banking/savings account.	_______.____

If you add your rental income to your general banking or savings account, then if you've counted it before when recording your savings or checking account then do not enter that amount below. You don't want to double count any earnings or income. However, if you keep those earnings in a separate account then enter that amount above in **(2r)**.

Collectibles & Antiques

Collectibles are objects suitable for a collection. While the word was originally synonymous with works of fine art and antiques, it now includes items collected as a hobby, for display, or as an investment whose value may appreciate.

If you purchased an antique or collectible with the intention of holding it for its value, waiting for it to appreciate in the short-term, then you will pay Zakat on the total value of the collectible or antique. If you are holding it for the long term and it does not have a constant market value, meaning its value is determined upon appraisal and finalized upon sale, then you will pay Zakat on the total of its sale price when you sell, similar to other illiquid assets here. Add that value to **2s below**.

Please fill in the

2s – Aggregate value of collectibles and antiques:	________._____

Investment in privately held companies

If you've invested in a privately held company, and startup, or small business that is not publicly traded, then you will treat that investment based on the information available to you at the time your Zakat is due. If for example there has not been a liquidity or dissolution event, then you will treat this investment like an illiquid asset and not pay Zakat on it until the actual value is known through one of the above events.

If your investment has experienced an event, then depending on the type the ruling will differ:

- A Liquidity Event is an acquisition, merger, initial public offering (IPO), or other action that allows founders and early investors in a company to cash out some or all of their ownership shares.
    - In this case, if you do cash out you will pay 2.5% of the received value, and
    - if you receive shares, you will treat them like the passive investment in shares described above.
- A Dissolution Event occurs when a company voluntarily terminates its operations or when its creditors force the company to terminate its operations.

- o If you receive a settlement or payout from the dissolution, then you will pay 2.5% on the total value received.
- o If you do not receive anything from the dissolution or your rights remaining in litigation, then you will not pay any Zakat.
- o If eventually you receive nothing, then no Zakat it due.

Depending on the situation above, enter that value into **Aggregate value of a privately held investment (2t)**.

Please fill in the

2t – Aggregate value of a privately held investment:	_________.____

Crypto Currencies and Digital Assets

For the purposes of Zakat, Cryptocurrency is treated as any other currency is treated, like gold and silver. Because it is a currency and you are holding it because it is a currency, then you must pay Zakat on it. If you were holding the same amount of value for the same purpose at the time of the Prophet, do you have any doubt that you would be liable to pay Zakat on it? I personally have no doubt that you would have to, because the reasons for you holding it and the reasons for having to pay Zakat on Gold are exactly the same. It is a store of value accepted for payment by a broad community of people.

A majority of scholars, both classically and in the modern period, held that if a currency not found during the Prophet's time functions exactly like how gold and silver function, then we treat them the same. We apply the same rules to it: so just as it would be Riba to loan out our gold for interest, we don't loan out our crypto for interest. Similarly, just as we pay Zakat on your savings in gold, we pay it on crypto.

How do I determine the value of my Crypto for Zakat Purposes?

Before we start, please note: the tokens and amounts below are simply for illustration purposes, to show you how to do the calculations. Do not simply take the values below for your Zakat calculations without reviewing whether or not the values have changed.

That said, when determining the value of crypto, you can take one of two approaches:

1. Convert the value of your crypto
    a. Either convert it to your local currency, then add that amount to your total assets. Essentially, you're treating your crypto like your local currency, then your local currency like gold or silver, then paying your Zakat in your local currency.
    b. If you use gold for your Niṣāb, convert the value of your crypto to a gold tethered precious metal token, like Tether Gold (XAUt) or PAX Gold (PAXG) tokens.[18]

---

[18] - The PAXG token website states, "PAX Gold (PAXG) is a digital asset. Each token is backed by one fine troy ounce (t oz) of a 400 oz London Good Delivery gold bar, stored in Brink's vaults. If you own PAXG, you own the underlying physical gold, held in custody by Paxos Trust Company." For more information see the Paxos website. (URL: https://paxos.com/paxgold/, last accessed: 03/12/2022)

      i. Each of these tokens is equal to one (1) troy ounce, and one (1) troy ounce is worth 31.10 grams.

      ii. 85 grams of gold as Niṣāb divided by 31.10 grams per token equals 2.73 PAXG tokens.

      iii. Therefore, your Niṣāb in PAXG gold backed crypto tokens each worth one (1) troy ounce would be 2.73 tokens.

c. If you use silver for your Niṣāb, convert the value of your crypto to a silver tethered precious metal token, something like SilverToken (SLVT).[19]

      i. Each of these tokens is equal to 1.035692 ounces which equals 29.36 grams.

      ii. 595 grams of gold as Niṣāb divided by 29.36 grams per token equals 4.5 tokens.

      iii. Therefore, your Niṣāb in silver backed SLVT crypto tokens each worth

---

[19] - Per the SilverToken site, the current ratio is 1.035692 oz. of Silver = 1 SLVT. The SilverToken Ratio is calculated by dividing the amount of vaulted silver by the number of SilverTokens in circulation plus the number of SilverTokens in the reserve account to represent all SilverDollars SLVD in circulation. (URL: https://silvertoken.com/faq, last accessed: 03/12/2022)

1.035692 ounces would be 20.26 tokens.

2. Therefore, if your crypto is equal or greater than:

    a. The value of 85 grams of gold in your local currency, then add the cash value to your other assets and pay 2.5% on your assets.

    b. If you want to pay Zakat from your cryptocurrency directly, then convert to a precious metal backed token as shown above

        i. If gold, then use PAXG: If equal to or greater than 2.73 tokens, pay 2.5% of the value of your wallet.

        ii. If silver, then use SLVT: If equal to or greater than 20.26 tokens, pay 2.5% of the value of your wallet.

3. If you've had a consistent value greater than the value of 85 grams of gold / 2.73 PAXG gold backed tokens or 595 grams of silver / 20.26 SLVT silver backed tokens in your wallet on the month's end for an entire 12 months, then you will pay 2.5% of Zakat on the total value of your wallet.

4. Pay 2.5% of your cryptocurrency in Zakat for the year.

    a. If your wallet has 20 ETH, then you own the equivalent of 25.77 PAXG tokens. Pay 0.5 ETH as 2.5% of your Zakat.

b. If you take the USD value, then you have $51,488.50, and 2.5% of that would be $1287.21 USD.

An easy way to do this is the go to a swap exchange like Uniswap and enter in your cryptocurrency holdings converted to PAXG. You'll see the PAXG value, as well as the USD value instantly.

Remember however, that you have to pay Zakat on full value of the converted amount, not just gains since you bought it. You also should not be deducting conversion fees or transfer costs. Zakat must be paid from the gross amount calculated. If you need to transfer it to someone else or incur a cost in paying it, that comes out of your pocket. The sum total of Zakat is the right of the poor, and therefore has to be paid in total as is.

Please fill in the

2u – Aggregate value of Crypto:	_________._____

What are NFTs?

A Non-Fungible Token (NFT) gives you something that can't be copied. NFTs can be used for real estate, contracts, and a number of other things. NFTs give you ownership of the work. And that means if someone else uses it, you can charge them royalties etc.

To put it in terms of physical art: Anyone can buy a print of Van Gogh's starry night, but only one person can own the original. So, I don't own this painting and I don't have digital rights to make money off of its use.

NFTs are a digital means for proving the ownership of an asset, like your car's title proves you own it. Add to that with an NFT, you can also track who has owned that digital asset in the past and what was done with it, just like getting a Carfax tells you the history of your car's sale and repair. Now imagine that you signed your car up for Turo, so that you could rent it out when you're not using it. NFTs track who used it and how much money they have to pay you as well, in addition to transferring the money they owe to you automatically.

For the most part, NFTs right now are being used as overpriced collectibles on the internet. As they progress, you'll find more sophisticated ways of documenting, selling, and licensing the use of assets. I am long the idea of NFTs as a technology solution, short the idea that a JPG is worth millions of dollars.[20]

Are NFTs permissible to own and trade?

The short answer is: Yes, as long as the digital asset is permissible. So, when buying an NFT, you'll need to

---

[20] - For more on this topic, see: "NFTs: Non-Fungible Tokens – A Very Simple Explanation" (URL: https://www.joebradford.net/nfts-non-fungible-tokens-a-very-simple-explanation/, last accessed: 03/01/2022)

look at what the subject matter is and what its use/purpose is. If it is permitted, then purchasing the NFT to buy and hold or to trade for profit is permitted. The important thing you need remember is to not waste money on overpriced, hyped up goods!

Zakat on crypto, LP tokens, utility tokens, and NFTs?

Zakat is due on any cryptocurrency or token you hold. The question is, when and why? If you hold the coin as currency and there are no staking rewards or dividends related to it, then you pay on the value of the coin like you would currency. If you hold the coin as currency and there staking rewards or dividends that are earned, then you will pay Zakat on value of the coin and any rewards distributed as well.

If you hold a token in a project, and the token is *not* used as a fungible currency but simply a representation of your investment in an ongoing project, like an LP token, you will pay on the dividends you receive from the token. When you sell the LP token, you'll pay on the sales price as well, without deducting any expenses or liabilities. As for Zakat on NFTs, we'll cover that next.

How to treat NFTs based on their underlying assets

As for NFTs, how and if you'll pay Zakat on them is based on what their underlying asset is. Remember, an

NFT is simply a container for holding and controlling a unique asset.

How you pay Zakat on an NFT is dependent on what that NFT represents:

- If the underlying asset controlled by the NFT is art, then you would treat the NFT exactly like art mentioned earlier.
- If the NFT controls real estate, you will pay on the NFT as you would real estate.
- If the NFT is a collectible, then you will treat it as collectibles.
- If your NFT pays rewards or dividends, then you will pay on the rewards and dividends.

Please fill in the

2v – Aggregate value of LP Token Dividends*: * Exclude if already included with cash, banking/savings account.	___________.______
2w – Aggregate value of NFTs*: * Remember this depends on what the NFT underlying asset is.	
2x – Aggregate value of Sales price of LP Token of NFT held for trade.	

Business Inventory

If you are a businessperson whose business sells inventory, then that business inventory is one of two types:

> **A)** Inventory that was previously for sale but now is unable to be sold.[21]

> **B)** Inventory that is designated for sale and is not under contract.

As for category A), then you will treat them exactly as you dealt with illiquid assets above. In the case of category B) however, if you have outstanding inventory that is up for sale and is not under contract, then you must pay Zakat on the value of that inventory.

Samura b. Jundub says, "We were ordered to give our Ṣadaqa from the inventory we present for sale." Abu Dawūd narrated this in his Sunan.

You will need to tally your inventory not under contract and pay Zakat on that. If your inventory is under contract, then you've essentially already sold it, and you'll count that money earned from those contracts as "Accounts Receivable." When the receivables from those

---

[21] - This is sometimes referred to as "dead stock" or "obsolete inventory."

sales come in, the cash value will be added to your current account and Zakat paid on cash.

If your inventory is not under contract, meaning it is just sitting on a shelf waiting to be sold, then you'll calculate the **Aggregate Cash value of inventory (2y)**.

Here's an example:

Abdullah owns a packaging supply company. He has a warehouse of bubble-wrap that holds 500 rolls of bubble-wrap. 350 rolls of that bubble-wrap are under contract to all local post offices, they just pick it up at different times and pay quarterly. The remaining 150 rolls are there for one-off sales and walk-ins. Each roll sells for one hundred dollars ($100.^{00}). That's an aggregate value of 15,000.^{00} USD. This is the amount that you will add to your Zakat calculation.

There is one thing that you need to remember when calculating Zakat on your business inventory. Remember to differentiate between the types of sales you are in. If you are in retail sales, use the retail value. If you are a wholesaler, then write down the wholesale price. In the previous example, if you sell each roll for $85.00 USD then you'll pay Zakat on 85,000.00 USD as the cash value of your inventory.

There is one advantage to paying Zakat on your business inventory that you may find useful. If you sell a product and giving a Zakat recipient that product is better for them than cash, then you can give your Zakat in the form of that product. Let's say you sell automobile tires, foodstuff, or some other consumable product. Pay in kind and you can provide someone with a new set of tires or groceries, for example.

Take a moment to fill in the aggregate value of your inventory not under contract and has been with you for one year or more.

Please fill in the:

2y – Aggregate Cash Value of Inventory:	_________._____

Accounts Receivables

If you run a small business, are a sole proprietor, or are a partner in a company, you probably know what accounts receivable are. "Accounts Receivable" is an amount of money owed by customers to your business in exchange for goods and services provided. The only difference is, they have not paid for them yet, but can and will by a certain date. Some companies will allow their customers 30, 60, or 90 days to pay for goods and services rendered. Because the customer can pay, yet you have allowed them to pay you later, the exact same logic applied to "Good Debt" mentioned in the last section applies here to Accounts Receivable.

If you have **Accounts Receivable (2z)** in your balance sheet, then include the amount that you will receive in line 2s below.

Please fill in

2z – Accounts Receivable:	________.____

I doubt you are a farmer

Zakat is obligatory on livestock and crop yields with certain conditions. If you own sheep, goat, cows, or camels of certain numbers and they are free-range, grazing animals then you are obliged to pay Zakat on a per head basis. This has a very specific detailed schedule to follow for free grazing animals. We will not cover this here because most people are in no need of this information. Similar to livestock, if you own a farm and have constant crop yields, there are specific amounts that you need to pay at harvest. If you are a farmer and need this information, please contact me.

If, however, you own animals, but they are not free-range grazing animals of the types mentioned above then:

a) if you keep them penned for personal use, such as dairy cattle, or you have a small herd of sheep raised in pens, <u>there is no Zakat to pay on them at all.</u>

b) If you keep cattle, sheep, or any other animal for sale (meaning you are a livestock supplier of some sort) then you'll treat them exactly like business inventory, calculating their cash value and paying Zakat on the **Value of livestock for sale (2aa).**

Please fill in the

2aa –Value of livestock for sale:	________.______

Debt: The good of it and the bad of it

Does someone owe you money? Are you able to collect that money right now? If so, this is known as good debt. Let me give you an example:

Your mother asks to borrow $500 to pay a bill. She promises that as soon as she gets paid, she'll wire the money to you. On payday, she calls asking for your account details. You tell her: That's ok, Mom. Just keep that $500 with you, and whenever I am in the area, I will pick it up.

This loan that you chose not to collect on from your mother is "good debt." Money owed to you that you can collect on is treated the same as cash in hand.

Unless something prevents you from doing so, like the inability of the person to pay or their refusal to pay, then you are liable to pay Zakat on it. If this is the case, this amount is considered "bad debt." In short, you only pay on accessible cash flow, and good debt fits that description. For bad debt, then you pay on it whenever you actually receive it, as described above in "Illiquid Assets."

If you have **Good debt that you can collect on (2bb)**, please fill in that amount below:

Please fill in

2bb – Good debt that you can collect on:	__________.____

Worksheet #1: Total Earnings and Income

Add up the amounts in each section, then total them on the next page.

Cash and Cash Equivalents	
2a - Cash on Hand	_________.____
2b – Checking Account	_________.____
2c – Saving Account	_________.____
2d – Silver in grams _________.____	
A - Price of silver per gram _________.____	
Multiply the # of Grams by line A	_________.____
2e – Gold in grams _________.____	
B - Price of gold per gram _________.____	
Multiply the # of Grams by line B	_________.____
Cash Subtotal	_________.____
Investments	
2f – Aggregate value of actively traded shares	_________.____
2g – CRI Zakat Liable Amount:	
2h – Zakat Liable Dividend Amount	
2i – Aggregate Cash out Price of long-term shares	
2j – post Tax 401k distributions	_________.____
2k – post Tax IRA distributions	_________.____
2l – post Tax ESA withdrawals	_________.____
2m – post Tax 529 withdrawals	_________.____
2n – Aggregate Amount of HSA account	_________.____
Investments Subtotal	_________.____

Illiquid Assets (Art, Real Estate, Etc.)	
2o – Sales Price of Artwork you sold this year:	________._____
2p –Market Value of Real Estate active on the market:	________._____
2q –Value received from sale of inactive property:	_______._____
2r – Aggregate value of rental income*: * Exclude if already included with cash, banking/savings account.	________._____
2s – Aggregate value of collectibles and antiques:	________.____
2t – Aggregate value of a privately held investment:	________.____
2u – Aggregate value of Crypto:	________.____
2v – Aggregate value of LP Token Dividends*: * Exclude if already included with cash, banking/savings account.	________.____
2w - Aggregate value of NFTs*: * Remember this depends on what the NFT underlying asset is.	________.____
2x – Aggregate value of Sales price of LP Token of NFT held for trade.	________.____
2y – Aggregate Cash Value of Inventory:	________.____
2z – Accounts Receivable:	________.____
2aa –Value of livestock for sale:	________._____
2bb – Good debt that you can collect on:	________._____
Illiquid Assets Subtotal	________.____

Business Inventory and debt/receivables	
2s – Aggregate Value of Inventory:	_______.____
2t – Accounts Receivable:	_______.____
2u –Value of livestock for sale:	_______.____
2v – Good debt you can collect on:	_______.____
2w – Principal on Fixed Income instruments (remember to add this from page 93):	_______.____
Inventory/receivables Subtotal	_______.____

Totals	
Cash Subtotal	_______.____
Investments Subtotal	_______.____
Real Estate Subtotal	_______.____
Inventory/receivables Subtotal	_______.____
Grand Total (A)	_______.____

This grand total (A) is your aggregate earnings and income before deducting Haram earnings and deducting expenses. Make note of this amount for later.

IV - Haram earnings

This section will deal with impermissible earnings from two very common asset classes:

- Equity investments
- Fixed Income instruments (like bonds)

After this we will look at two common questions:

- Do I pay zakat on haram wealth?
- What do I do with interest or impermissible income after I've calculated it?

Haram Earnings on Equity Investments

If you are invested in the stock market, a 401k, an IRA, or similar, then the shares and funds that you invest in should be permissible. You should avoid investing in sectors whose primary earning activities are centered on one of the following:

1) Alcohol, Tobacco, & drugs.
2) Gambling & betting operations.
3) Cinema, Adult entertainment, Advertising, & media.
4) Conventional financial services.
5) Defense & weapons manufacturing.
6) Food & Beverage sectors involved in the sale of prohibited items, like pork & alcoholic beverages.

As long as a company's primary earnings activities are permitted, if it engages in any secondary earnings activities that are forbidden or are questionable, it is still permitted to invest in it as long as the secondary earnings are less than 5% of total revenues. Although scholars made an exception for investing in companies like these[22], these earnings need to be purified. Any gains from impermissible secondary earning must be purified because they were made from Haram activities in order to absolve yourself of the sin of your wealth being involved in something forbidden, even if you did not intend to do so.

To find out if the stocks you own have impermissible earnings, you'll need to read the balance sheets of the company, the 10K, as well as any earnings reports that the company issues. Once you are certain of the total of your impermissible income, you can then absolve yourself of it by using one of two methods to calculate the impermissible earnings.

#1: Earnings on Equities without a Dividend Distribution

If you are actively invested in the stock market, meaning you are:

1) actively involved in swing trading or day trading, or

---

[22] - The AAOIFI standards for example, state that this allowance is the exception, not the rule.

2) you are in a buy and hold position but will sell when an opportunity arises,

then you will use the following formula for your equities that do not pay a dividend distribution:

$$\left(\frac{Total\ Prohibited\ Income + Interest}{No.\ of\ Shares\ Issued}\right) * No.\ of\ Shares\ Owned$$

Look to the "Income Statement" of the company you own, then see if there are entries for "Other Income" or "Interest Income". Take this amount and gather the other information needed for the calculation above.

For example, if you own one thousand (1000) shares of ticker HD, which is Home Depot, then their revenue sources are for the most part permissible, except that they have 0.04% non-compliant income from Interest Income. At the time of writing this, this amounted to above 47 million dollars. Home Depot also has 1.04B outstanding shares at this time.

$$\left(\frac{\$47,000,000}{1,040,000,000}\right) * 1000\ Shares\ Owned =$$

This gives us 4.5 cents per share, and because we own one thousand shares, our total Haram earnings from our HD shares would total $45.00. After calculating this amount for the shares, you own, add it this to **Haram Earnings on Equities (3a)** below.

#2: Earnings on the Dividend Distribution

If you receive a dividend distribution from the stock you own, then you will need to calculate the prohibited income for the capital gains on the market value of the stock as well as calculate the percentage of the dividend from impermissible earnings. Use the following formula on that dividend amount:

$$\left(\frac{Prohibited\ Income}{Total\ Income}\right) * Dividend\ Recieved$$

HD also pays a dividend. Using this calculation above, we would look to the Income Statement again. HS has total income of 132.16 billion dollars. They also pay a dividend of 1.90 per share per quarter. How much are the Haram earnings on dividends per share?

$$\left(\frac{47,000,000}{132.16\ billion}\right) * 1.90 = .0004 \text{ cents per share}$$

Remember that dividends are paid monthly, quarterly, or yearly. In the case of HD, the dividend is paid quarterly. Which means we need to multiply the Haram earnings on the dividend by four, then multiply by the number of shares we own.

$$(Haram\ Earnings\ Per\ Share * Interval) * \#\ of\ shares$$

This gives us the following result:

$$(.0004 * 4 \ Quarters) * 1000 \ shares = \ 2.70$$

Therefore, if you were paid a dividend on shares owned, calculate this amount as shown above and then add this to **Haram Earnings on dividends (3b)** below.

Please fill in the:

3a – Haram Earnings on Equities:	_________._____
3b – Haram Earnings on dividends:	_________._____

Haram Earnings on Fixed Income Instruments

Bonds are debt instruments. An investor will loan money to a corporation or government that borrows the funds for a defined period of time with the agreement to return the principal and interest according to a fixed interest rate[23]. There is near consensus of modern scholars that bonds are impermissible, as "every loan which draws a benefit is Ribā". This rule is a universally applicable principle among scholars. Fixed income instruments are considered impermissible interest (Ribā) and you must absolve yourself of any Haram earnings.

To determine how to calculate the Haram earnings on a bond you own, the first thing we need to do is look back to how you came to own that bond in the first place:

Situation One: You purchased a fixed income instrument willfully then realized that it was wrong

If you purchased the bond willingly but did not know that doing so was impermissible, then in this case you must deduct the principal you paid for it, and the rest of the earnings you must absolve yourself of. So, for example, if you purchased a bond for $100 and it has accrued earnings of $5, then you should sell it and give the $5 of earnings away to charity. Add the $100 dollars

---

[23] - See www.investopedia.com for more.

to your Earnings in **Principal on Fixed Income instruments (2v)** below and the $5 dollars to your purification amount in **Value of Bond Earnings (3c)** below.

Situation Two: You were given a fixed income instrument as a gift

If you were given a bond or similar instrument as a gift (like many people receive while young from relatives as birthday gifts) then you still should sell it, however in this case you can keep both the principal and earnings from the bond sale. Why? Because you were not the original purchaser of the bond and are not liable for the sin of having originally purchased it. Example: If you were given a bond as a child with a face value of $100 dollars, but then as an adult realize that you should not be holding fixed income willfully, then sell the bond and count the sales price as principal in line 2u below.

Situation Three: You are required by law, regulation, or an employer to hold fixed income instruments

The last situation is where you are invested in a fund where you have no choice but to allocate towards fixed income. Your employer may not give you a choice in your 401k or IRA, or maybe you don't have enough money to create an SDA (Self Directed Account) and then switch to equities.

In this case, you'll calculate **Principal on Fixed Income instruments**, adding that to line **2v** below. Then add the earnings on that allocation to your purification amount in line 3c below.

Please fill in the

2w – Principal on Fixed Income instruments: *remember to add this to the earnings worksheet on page 85*	_______.____
3c –Value of Bond Earnings:	(_______.____)

What do I do with Haram earnings?

Ibn Ḥibbān narrates from Abu Huraira that the Prophet ﷺ said[24]:

> When you've given the Zakat of your wealth then you have fulfilled your obligation. Whoever gathered impermissible wealth then gave it in charity will have no reward for doing so and its sin will be upon him.

Based on this hadith, all scholars both past and present agree that it is imperative to absolve oneself of any Haram earnings. Regardless of whether those earnings

---

[24] - Ibn Ḥibbān, al-Ṣaḥīḥ, #3216.

are from interest bearing accounts, business transactions, or investments.

As for who you should pay this money to, to be considered absolved of these impermissible earnings, there are three approaches:

1) It should be used for public welfare projects, like civic improvements (public restrooms, parking lots, and similar).
2) It should only be used for the Poor and Indigent (the first two categories of Zakat recipients).
3) It may be used for any of the 8 categories of Zakat recipients.

There is no hard fast rule for which of these three approaches is preferred. However, I advise my clients to give to charities that service the poor, homeless, and hungry in their area.

Worksheet #2: Haram Earnings

Please fill in the:

3a – Haram Earnings on Equity investments:	__________.______
3b – Haram Earnings on Equity dividends:	__________.______
3c – Value of Bond Earnings:	__________.______
2w – Principal on Fixed Income instruments:	__________.______
Total Haram Earnings:	__________.______

V – Expenses and Liabilities

This is the month of your Zakat,
so pay the debts you owe to
others, then pay your Zakat.
~ ʿUthmān b. ʿAffān

Before paying your Zakat, take your family into consideration. While charity is praiseworthy, you have the obligation to take care of yourself and your family first. Prophet ﷺ Muhammad ﷺ said, "The upper hand is better than the lower hand but begin with those you are accountable for." In this section, we'll talk about how to count your monthly expenses, debts, and liabilities.

Monthly Living Expenses

When calculating your expenses and liabilities, you'll need to find out what you owe to others before you pay your Zakat. Because your bills and expenses are considered debts owed to others, you have to pay those first. Key thing to remember here is that you will only deduct from your total assets those debts, expenses, etc. that are immediately due.

What do I mean by "immediately due?" I mean that if you pay your mortgage monthly, you'll deduct one month of your mortgage payment if it's due. If you pay your car insurance monthly, same thing. What about your homeowner's insurance? If you pay it monthly, deduct one month. If you pay quarterly, then one quarter. If you pay it yearly, you can deduct one year.

The same goes for property taxes; if you pay them monthly and they are due this month, deduct one month. If your time to pay Zakat came right before you were going to pay your yearly property taxes, then deduct one year. If you have any delinquent tax payments you owe the government, include those as well.

All of this of course with the caveat that you are paying your Zakat at the same time these expenses are due. If you owe someone money and they want their money now, then you deduct that amount as well. Other expenses that can be deducted are rent, medical expenses (other than your insurance premium), groceries, transportation costs, and all other similar expenses *that are due immediately*.

Take a look at the worksheet on the next page and fill in your different expenses:

Please fill in

4a – Monthly Living Expenses:	
Monthly Mortgage or Rental Payment	(_______.___)
Medical Expenses	(_______.___)

Groceries, Energy, Telecom	(________.____)
Transportation, Petrol, upkeep	(________.____)
Miscellaneous Living Expenses	(________.____)
Total Monthly Living Expenses:	(________.____)
4b – Periodic Insurance Payments:	
Home /Renter's Insurance	(________.____)
Auto Insurance	(________.____)
Medical Insurance	(________.____)
Total Insurance Payments for the period:	(________.____)

Debts you owe to others

We started this section with a quote from ʿUthmān b. ʿAffān about paying debt before paying Zakat. Why pay your debts before paying Zakat? Well, God is merciful. Man is not. When we have been trusted enough to borrow from others, we should be trustworthy enough to pay those back. While God is merciful and forgiving, man is not and may demand his rights from us on the Day of Judgment. Therefore, you pay your debts to man first, as God has "commanded you to relay trusts to those that own them." (Quran 4:58)

If you owe someone money and that debt has become due, whether individually or as a business, then you must pay them before paying your Zakat.

Please fill in

4g – Debts you owe to others:	(_______.____)
	(_______.____)
	(_______.____)
Total	(_______.____)

Worksheet #3: Expenses and Liabilities

4a – Monthly Living Expenses:	(________.____)
4b – Insurance Payments:	(________.____)
4c – Property Tax Payments:	(________.____)
4d – Delinquent Tax Payments:	(________.____)
4e – Miscellaneous Fines:	(________.____)
4g – Debts you owe to others:	(________.____)
Total Expenses and Liabilities:	(________.____)

Part Three: Who to Give to & When to Give

VI - Giving Zakat

*What great people are the
poor! They carry our
provisions to the next life
without pay, placing them on
the scales in front of God!
~ al-Fudhayl ibn Iyaadh*

Zakat is a means to make a difference in people's lives. When giving you need to know three things:

1- Who not to give Zakat to?
2- Who to give it to?
3- Who is it best to give to?

Who should I NOT give my Zakat to?

There are five categories of people not eligible for Zakat:

(1) The rich
(2) The able-bodied worker
(3) Family Members
(4) The Family of the Prophet ﷺ
(5) Can Zakat be given to Non-Muslims?

We'll cover each in the following pages.

(1) The rich

Abu Dawūd narrates from Abdullah ibn Amr that the Prophet ﷺ said: "Zakat is not permissible for the rich, nor the able bodied & capable."

Abu Dawūd also narrates from Abu Saʿīd that the Messenger ﷺ said: "Zakat is not permissible for a rich man except in God's path, the way-farer, or in the case of a poor neighbor who receives something then gives it as a gift to you or invites you over."

(2) The able-bodied worker

In addition to the previous hadith, Abu Dawūd narrates from ʿUbaidillah b. ʿAdi that: "Two men informed him that they came to the Prophet ﷺ while he was distributing Zakat. He looked them up and down and saw that they were strong, so he said, "if you wish, I can give you something, but rich people and able-bodied earners have no share in it.""

There are several conditions for a person to be considered able-bodied and capable of earning:

1. Employment opportunities should be present.
2. That the employment be permissible.
3. That he/she be capable of performing such job without undue hardship.
4. That the job provides enough pay for basic needs (including that of dependents).

(3) Immediate Family Members

There is consensus that giving a family member whom you are responsible for supporting is not permitted. If you are responsible for maintaining someone financially, such as your parents, your wife, or your children, then you may not give them Zakat. Some scholars made exceptions for needy family members, but stipulated a degree of separation, such as a married daughter who is poor. Her maintenance and support are her husband's responsibility, but that does not mean that she is not needy. Her parents or siblings would be responsible to maintain her had she not been married, and so in her time of need they have more responsibility to give to her. They allowed for Zakat to be used for this purpose.

As for spouses, the following hadith narrated by al-Bukhari applies here. Zainab, wife of Abdullah b. Masʿūd, sent a question to the Prophet ﷺ about giving her Zakat to maintain her husband and some orphans in her custody, to which he answered that she "will get the reward of charity and the reward of kinship." Because the wife is not responsible to maintain the husband, her zakat is permissible if he is needy.

As for giving Zakat to family members other than those mentioned, then any family member whose maintenance you are not responsible for may be given Zakat.

(4) The Family of the Prophet ﷺ

Muslim narrates from ʿAbdulMuttalib b. Rabīʿah that the Prophet ﷺ said: "These offerings are only the filth of the people, they are not permissible for Muhammad nor the family of Muhammad."

The family of Prophet ﷺ here includes all of Banu Hāshim and Banu Muttalib.

(5) Can Zakat be given to Non-Muslims?

There is general agreement that Zakat is not to be given to anyone who is fighting against Islam and Muslims. [25] As for other non-Muslims who are non-combatants and do not hold animosity towards Muslims, there are three main opinions on this topic:

1. Non-Muslims are never eligible for Zakat, not even the category for "softening the hearts."
2. Non-Muslims may only be given from the category for "softening the hearts." This is the majority opinion.
3. Non-Muslims may be given from all categories of Zakat as long as a need exists and that fulfilling

---

[25] - See Ibn al-Mundhir, Kitab al-Ijma'.

that need will not deprive poor Muslims from assistance in their own communities.

I have written about this topic in other places and advise you to read those articles to make an informed decision.

Who can I give my Zakat to?

Those for whom Zakat is paid for the account of are enumerated in the sixtieth verse of Surah al-Tawbah:

> "Charity is only paid for: the destitute, the poor, those collecting it, to soften the hearts; in manumission, those in debt, in God's path, and the wayfarer; an obligation from God. God is Omniscient, All-Wise."

From this verse we can deduce eight categories that Zakat may be paid to:

1) The destitute (al-Fuqaraʾā).
2) The poor (al-Masākīn).
3) Those collecting it (al-ʿāmilīna ʿalaihā).
4) To soften the hearts (al-muʾallafat qulūbuhum).
5) In manumission (fi ʾl-riqāb).
6) Those in debt (al-Ghārimīn).
7) In God's path (fi sabīlillah).
8) The wayfarer (Ibn ʾl-sabīl).

Let's discuss each of these eight categories.

Category #1 & #2: The indigent and the poor

What is the exact difference between a poor person and an indigent person? Al-Bukhari narrates from Abu Hurairah:

> The poor man is not one who is sent off by a bite or two, or a date or two; the poor man is the one that does not find wealth that suffices him nor do most notice him and donate to him due to his abstention from asking people.

In simple terms, the poor person (Miskīn) is akin to the working poor who while in need does not ask or beg. If you saw them, you would not expect them to be needy. They may own property but cannot maintain their living expenses. When you are forced into a choice of whom to give your Zakat to, the person who has absolutely nothing and the person who has enough to get him by for a day or two, who will you give it to?

The rule of thumb here is: Any person that does not find sufficient means to live (for himself and/or dependents) may be given Zakat, regardless of the other forms of wealth they may possess.

When faced with a choice between two people, look for the person who is worse off.

Category #3: Those collecting it

This category exists to allow organizations and states the ability to hire qualified people to run the Zakat system, making it self-sufficient. This allows the collection and distribution of our charitable giving to not become a burden in and of itself.

Those employed in Zakat collection and distribution should meet certain key criteria: They should be mature, intelligent, trustworthy Muslims with knowledge of Zakat law and technical qualifications for the position. This person should also embody the requisite good character and professionalism expected from him or her. He should also be transparent in his dealings and prudent with the wealth he is entrusted to collect.

Noting that this category can become a loophole for people to abuse Zakat, Muslim jurists placed several conditions for the management of Zakat distribution:

1. The individuals employed are preferred to be from the poor and indigent looking for work.
2. Individuals employed are forbidden from accepting personal gifts while employed in collecting Zakat.
3. No more than 1/8 of the gross Zakat funds collected in that year should be used for paying those employed. If they are poor and the funds allocated in this category are not enough, the shortfall can be made up from other categories that apply to the person's needs.

4. The organization collecting and distributing Zakat should be one created solely for the purpose of charitable spending.[26]

Category #4: To soften the hearts

Preservation of faith is a main objective of Islam. This includes the faith of those already Muslim, those whose faith may be blossoming, and those who need to be opened up to the idea of Islam being acceptable. To protect the faith of these people is an objective of Islamic law.

Any act that would preserve a person's Islam or prevent Islam from being disparaged, would fall into this category. New convert programs, Early Learning programs, targeted Media campaigns to combat anti-Muslim sentiment, and similar are examples of how this category

---

[26] - Classically the category of "Those collecting" was managed by the state, and the Zakat collections were deposited in the state treasury or Bait al-Mal. In that absence of Bait al-Mal, is it possible for Masājid, Islamic Centers, and Daʿwa organizations to stand in? This is a debated question among scholars, and one where strict conditions must be implemented. Why? The conflict of interest found in both acting as a Zakat collection authority then simultaneously distributing it (spending it) on the same organization's expenses is blatantly obvious. To allow a person to both pose as the legitimate authority for Zakat collection while also claiming a need for Zakat, allows a lack of oversight and distortion of measuring of actual need that can lead to fraud, abuse, and misappropriation of Zakat funds. In communities around the world, Zakat funds are collected with the assumption they are being given to legitimate Zakat recipients, only for the same organization to turn around and spend the funds on tenuous expenses – things like Gala dinners, marketing, and construction costs – while the poor and needy in their areas go hungry.

If you do give to one of these types of organizations, make sure that they have a clear and transparent policy in place for how the Zakat funds are accounted for, that the funds designated for Zakat are held separate from general funds, that the recipients of those funds through the organization are eligible for Zakat, and that the organization clearly reports to the community how the funds are used and what types of people they are they are disbursed to. Anything less opens the organization up to criticism and open you, the one giving Zakat, up to the danger of your Zakat not having been accepted.

may be spent. Please keep in mind that such things should be approved by a qualified Zakat scholar to see if the organization or cause you want to give to qualifies. If an organization claims eligibility but does not have a third party vetting their claims, stay away.

Category #5: In manumission

Zakat should also be used to abolish all forms of human subjugation. It is important to note here that peonage, human trafficking, child labor, and slavery still exist in the modern world and most societies are guilty of illegal bondage, even Muslim ones. Al-Bukhari narrates from Abu Hurairah that the Prophet ﷺ said:

> God himself has said: Three people, I am their plaintiff on the Day of Judgment; a man that was given in my name yet was deceitful; a man that sold a free man and ate the price; and a man that hired someone, and whence he received full service, did not give him his pay.

Chattel slavery (the type that comes to mind for most western audiences) is forbidden in Islam, due to this hadith and many other texts.[27] Some examples of this in the modern world are the Zamīndāri Nizam in the Indian Sub-continent, farming peonage in the Southern United States, and child labor in Southeast Asia. Programs that

---

[27] - Any freeman that is robbed of that freedom is due reparations. Scholars of the Maliki School have stated that if a person was to sell a free man into slavery and it was not known where that person sold as a slave was, or if it was impossible to return him to his family, then the guilty party should have to pay the blood-wit (diyah) in total to that person's inheritors. See Al-Hattab, Mawahib al-Jalil, and 'Illish, Minah al-Jalil. The latter states this as the position of Imam Malik himself.

seek to free people from these situations are all eligible for assistance under this category of Zakat.

Category #6: Those in debt

Debtors are another category of people that Zakat should be used for. There are two types of debts eligible for Zakat: Debt incurred for personal expenditures and those incurred for a collective good.

1- Debts incurred for personal expenditures:

This includes debts of a person living paycheck to paycheck, holds monthly credit card debt, and generally spends all his earnings on living expenses because they never have enough money to make ends meet. Another example would be a person who incurred medical expenses that insurance would not cover. Assisting people with their bills, such as electricity, water, gas, and etcetera is also valid for Zakat.

There are several conditions for using Zakat to pay off a person's personal debts:

1. Lack of sufficient funds to settle the debt.
2. It was incurred for permissible ends (meaning they didn't go into debt because of gambling).
3. The debt is currently due.
4. If not paid the debt becomes a civil offense.

2- Debts incurred for a collective good:

The other debt that Zakat can be used for is debt incurred for a collective good; the following hadith collected by Muslim from Qabīsa ibn Mukhāriq applies here:

> God's Messenger said, "Begging is allowable only in one of three cases: A man who has become a guarantor for a payment, to whom begging is allowed till he receives that amount, after which he must stop; a man whose property has been destroyed by a calamity which has smitten him, to whom begging is allowed till he gets what will support life; and a man who has been smitten by poverty, the genuineness of which is confirmed by three intelligent members of his people, to whom begging is allowed till he receives what will support life. Any other reason for begging, Qabīsa, and the one who engages in such consumes it as a thing which is forbidden.

Included in this are people affected by natural disasters, being that such a person not only is considered poor, but usually must borrow money to get back on his feet.

Category #7: In God's path

When explaining the meaning of "In God's path", most medieval scholars specified this category as applying to those fighting in God's path, i.e., engaged in some form of armed, physical struggle for the victory of an Islamic nation.

There are conditions for Zakat to be given to such people: they must be non-conscripted soldiers, fighting under a legitimate sovereign Muslim ruler, and have no salary or stipend of their own. Think of it like this: If George Washington was a Muslim leader, then during the

Revolutionary War he could have used Zakat to pay the militias that helped fight alongside the Continental Army. If these conditions are not met, then Zakat is not paid for this purpose.

Some later scholars expanded this meaning, saying that any attempt to establish God's word as highest is eligible for this category. Jihad is many types, spanning personal struggles to armed resistance against oppression. In the Makkan period, the first type of Jihad mentioned in the Quran was the Jihad of the Quran, i.e., calling people to faith with God's book, good manners, and rational debate. This happened before any armed struggle existed. There is concurrence among scholars that if a means to call to God's path and persuade people's hearts exists, then armed resistance is not an option.[28]

To this group of scholars, the methods used to serve "in God's path" are numerous and given the generalities of the texts encompass more than just armed struggle and extend to every legitimate act that helps to promote Islam as God's highest word. And it needs to be said, that while this opinion is common, it cannot be left open ended. Consult with a scholar and Zakat expert to

---

[28] - Ibn Taymiya, al-Hisba.

determine whether or not this is applicable to a cause or person you would like to give Zakat to or not.

Category #8: The wayfarer

The wayfarer is a traveler who has left his land and does not have enough accessible money to return. The Quran encourages travel and free-trade and therefore the Islamic legal and social system should support those that fulfill that commandment, leaving their homes to become gainfully earning members of society.

In order for the wayfarer to be eligible for Zakat, he must fulfill the following conditions:

1. He must need assistance while in a state of instability or transience. A person that is out of cash but has a credit or debit card at their disposal, would not qualify.
2. His purpose of travel must not have been to sin. This would include not only those that are travelling for permissible reasons, but also those who are refugees or are exiled.
3. He must not have any means available to him. If he is rich but has no access to his wealth, he can be given enough Zakat to facilitate regaining access to his personal wealth.

Zakat Distribution Guidelines Summary

We can sum up the guidelines for distributing Zakat as follows:

- There is no clear cut or bright line rule for the amount to be given to an individual or a single category.
- The Poor and Destitute have more right to Zakat than the other categories.
- Those whose needs are more dire and numerous given precedence.
- When giving to the poor and indigent, it is better to empower them with training and tools than to simply hand out cash disbursements.
- For those collecting Zakat, they should be given a fair wage, but no more than 1/8 of the total collected.
- For Categories 4-8:
  - Zakat given to these categories is dictated by actual need and overall social benefit,
  - It should be paid on their behalf to their creditors or the services they need. It is not recommended to give cash directly.
  - They should exhibit need by providing bills, receipts, etc. of the expenses involved,

- o Even though these categories receive Zakat, social assistance of the less fortunate must not be neglected.

Best Practices When Giving

Many people ask, "How can I make the most of my Zakat?" What they are really pointing out is their need for a comprehensive stewardship plan that takes into consideration their spending, personal savings, Zakat, general Sadaqa (charity), and volunteer hours. My book on this topic covers most of what you would need to know to set up an all-inclusive plan for charitable giving (both financially and through volunteering)[29].

Since we are covering Zakat however, I want to draw your attention to several important points to consider:

- Maximizing your Tax deduction:
  - o If you are giving your Zakat to an organization, make sure you get a receipt and use that donation receipt when filing your taxes.
  - o This will free up more cash for you to use for your family and other charitable acts.
- If you work for a corporation, inquire about a corporate matching program when donating.

---

[29] - Islam, Stewardship, and the Divine Trust, forthcoming.

- o Each company has their own guidelines as to how much they will match, but the important thing to remember is if you are giving your Zakat to a non-profit, they will give money to that same non-profit as well.
  - o Some organizations match 1:1, some 2:1, and some even do 3:1 for special emergencies.
  - o It is a great opportunity to multiply your donation with minimal effort.
  - o Most large companies use services like EasyMatch which provide an intuitive and streamlined web-2.0'ish website to capture match requests.
- For personal donations, make sure that you develop a relationship with people in your communities.
- Take time to get to know your community.
  - o Many times, people complain to me about not knowing any poor in their communities. I've found that our busy schedules don't allow us the time to get to know people and their needs, so we are blind to the poor's presence in our communities.

If you have people or charities in mind, go ahead and fill in their names below:

Name 3 charities that you will give to, based on what you've read:

1)
____

2)
____

3)
____

Name 3 individuals that you will give to, based on what you've read:

1)
____

2)
____

3)
____

You can always fill these out later, but keep in mind that you'll need to give your Zakat to someone eligible, and its best to make a shortlist well beforehand so you are not rushed.

VII - Now Calculate Your Zakat!

Back in the beginning of this book we covered terms like "Ḥawl" and "Niṣāb." Now is the time to apply them. First thing we'll need to do is find out the minimum amount of money we have to have to be liable for Zakat. This is known as Niṣāb. In this book, we'll refer to it as Minimum Liable Amount (Niṣāb).

What do I mean by that? I mean that not everyone is liable for Zakat. Some people may have money, but that money is used for expenses throughout the year. Others may have savings, but that savings is not enough to make them liable for Zakat or is inaccessible to them. The Minimum Liable Amount (Niṣāb) is a floor used to measure whether or not you have to pay Zakat. If you have less than Niṣāb, you are not liable to pay Zakat. If you have more than Niṣāb, then you must pay it.

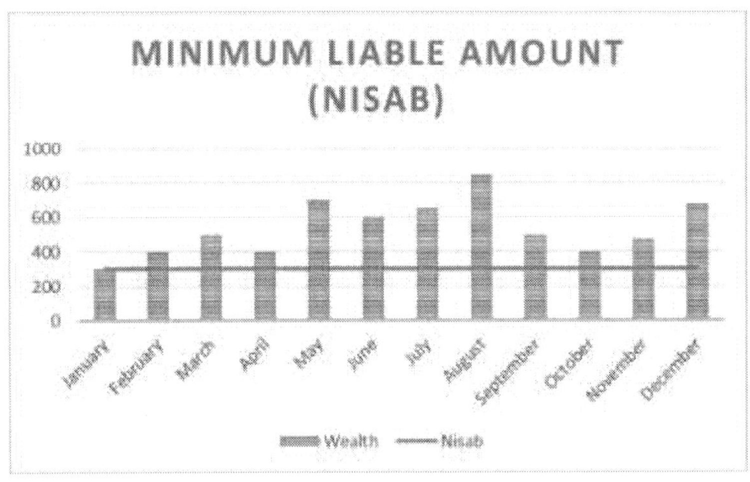

In the graphic above, our Minimum Liable Amount (Niṣāb) is $300 (just as an example). If this was your bank account, you'd look to see if you consistently have $300 or more of wealth liable for Zakat for a year. If you do, you'll pay on the entire amount in your account.

Think of it like a tax bracket. With standard tax deductions, if you earn $8,925 or less (filing single) you may not pay any taxes. If you earn anything above that, you'll pay 15% on the amount above $8,925. Zakat is different. Zakat is not progressive[30], it is similar to a flat tax. You pay your Zakat on your entire savings, not just the amount above the Minimum Liable Amount (Niṣāb).

If the MLA was $300, and you only have $250, then you won't pay Zakat. If for example you have $700, then you'll

---

[30] - Zakat is not progressive. To review this concept, see page 18.

pay 2.5% of 700 dollars, which is $17.50. You pay on the entire $700, not just the $400 above $300.

The amount below the Minimum Liable Amount is *included* in the total you pay Zakat on, do not exclude it. I reiterate this because many people make this common mistake when calculating their Zakat. Zakat is paid on the *total* amount; however, to be liable to pay Zakat you have to have equal to or more than the MLA (Niṣāb).

Find the Minimum Liable Amount (Niṣāb)

Now let's figure out what the Minimum Liable Amount (Niṣāb) is for today. First, we need to know today's price for a gram of Silver. There are several resources you can turn to for prices. I usually use a website known as www.silverpriceoz.com. This site can tell us the price per ounce, per gram, and per kilo. For the purposes of this section, all we need is the price per gram.

We'll take the spot price of silver (just to show you, you'll need to visit the above site and get the current amount).

- Price for 1 gram of silver = 0.53 USD
- Multiply that by 595 grams
- This gives an MLA (Niṣāb) of $315.35
- The cash value of the MLA (Niṣāb) of Silver is: 315.35 USD

What does this mean? It means that if you have 315.35 dollars or more in savings for one year or more, then you must pay Zakat on that amount.

Please fill in the price per gram of silver

X – Today's Price for 1 gram of silver	_______.____
Y – Multiply X by 595 grams:	_______.____
Z- the cash value of the MLA (Niṣāb) of silver is:	_______.____

Let's set our Zakat Year (Hawl)

Now, let's look back in your account history and determine if you've held this amount for more than one year.

- ☐ You start calculating the day your wealth is greater than the MLA (Niṣāb).
- ☐ If that amount remains constantly above the MLA (Niṣāb) for one year, you must pay Zakat on your total liable wealth.
- ☐ You can pay early, but only if you've reached Niṣāb[31].

---

[31] - If you pay early, and then realize your earnings projection is short (making your Zakat amount short) it is not permitted to claw back what you've paid early, but anything extra that you pay will be rewarded as charity.

The MLA (Niṣāb) this year is [insert line Z here]:	______________
Earliest date I have more than this amount is:	____/____/_____
One year from this date is:	____/____/_____
Was my savings greater than my MLA for the entirety of this period? Circle one:	Yes / No

Worksheet #4: Calculating your Zakat

A - Total Income and Earnings (from pg. 83):	_______.___
B - Total Haram Earnings (from pg. 95)	(______.___)
C - Permissible Wealth before deductions: [A minus B]	_______.___
D - Total expenses and liabilities (from pg. 100):	(______.___)
E – Total Wealth Liable for Zakat [C minus D]	_______.___
F – Minimum Liable Amount (Niṣāb) as of ______ (date)	_______.___
Is line E above greater than the amount in F?	YES/NO
Has line E been greater than line F for a year?	YES/NO
If you answered YES above, then multiply line E by 2.5%[32]. This is the total amount of Zakat you owe for this year.	_______.___

---

[32] - Many people use a date in the Islamic Calendar to calculate their Zakat, like Ramadan or Hajj. If you are using a date on the Gregorian calendar, then you need to multiply by 2.578 to make up for the additional 11 days difference between the two calendar years.

Actions Items:

I will give ________.____ in Zakat this year to the following charities/people:

1. ____________________________
2. ____________________________
3. ____________________________

I will absolve myself of ________.____ in Haram earnings this year giving it to the following charities/people:

1. ____________________________
2. ____________________________
3. ____________________________

Epilogue

My sincere hope is that this guide fulfilled its purpose and helped you in understanding and calculating your charitable giving. If you have any comments, questions, and (most importantly) corrections, please do not hesitate to contact me through my website www.JoeBradford.net. For your benefit, I've added an addendum with a copy of the four worksheets featured herein at the end of the book.

I hope this modest attempt at explaining one of the five pillars of Islam can be counted in my scales on the Day of Judgment. If there is anything good in this work, it is due to God's grace alone. If there are any mistakes, then it is from me alone.

And all praise is due to God, by whose grace good deeds are completed.

Joe Bradford
March 2022 / Shaʿbān 1443

Addendum: Extra Calculation Worksheets

Worksheet #1: Total Earnings and Income

Add up the amounts in each section, then total them on the next page.

Cash and Cash Equivalents	
2a - Cash on Hand	__________.____
2b – Checking Account	__________.____
2c – Saving Account	__________.____
2d – Silver in grams __________.____	
A - Price of silver per gram __________.____	
Multiply the # of Grams by line A	__________.____
2e – Gold in grams __________.____	
B - Price of gold per gram __________.____	
Multiply the # of Grams by line B	__________.____
Cash Subtotal	__________.____
Investments	
2f – Aggregate value of actively traded shares	__________.____
2g – CRI Zakat Liable Amount:	
2h – Zakat Liable Dividend Amount	
2i – Aggregate Cash out Price of long-term shares	
2j – post Tax 401k distributions	__________.____
2k – post Tax IRA distributions	__________.____
2l – post Tax ESA withdrawals	__________.____
2m – post Tax 529 withdrawals	__________.____
2n – Aggregate Amount of HSA account	__________.____
Investments Subtotal	__________.____

Illiquid Assets (Art, Real Estate, Etc.)	
2o – Sales Price of Artwork you sold this year:	________.____
2p –Market Value of Real Estate active on the market:	________.____
2q –Value received from sale of inactive property:	________.____
2r – Aggregate value of rental income*: * Exclude if already included with cash, banking/savings account.	________.____
2s – Aggregate value of collectibles and antiques:	________.____
2t – Aggregate value of a privately held investment:	________.____
2u – Aggregate value of Crypto:	________.____
2v – Aggregate value of LP Token Dividends*: * Exclude if already included with cash, banking/savings account.	________.____
2w - Aggregate value of NFTs*: * Remember this depends on what the NFT underlying asset is.	________.____
2x – Aggregate value of Sales price of LP Token of NFT held for trade.	________.____
2y – Aggregate Cash Value of Inventory:	________.____
2z – Accounts Receivable:	________.____
2aa –Value of livestock for sale:	________.____
2bb – Good debt that you can collect on:	________.____
Illiquid Assets Subtotal	________.____

Business Inventory and debt/receivables	
2s – Aggregate Value of Inventory:	_________.____
2t – Accounts Receivable:	_________.____
2u –Value of livestock for sale:	_________.____
2v – Good debt you can collect on:	_________.____
2w – Principal on Fixed Income instruments (remember to add this from page 93):	_________.____
Inventory/receivables Subtotal	_________.____

Totals	
Cash Subtotal	_________.____
Investments Subtotal	_________.____
Real Estate Subtotal	_________.____
Inventory/receivables Subtotal	_________.____
Grand Total (A)	_________.____

Worksheet #2: Haram Earnings

Please fill in the:

3a – Haram Earnings on Equity investments:	________.____
3b – Haram Earnings on Equity dividends:	________.____
3c – Value of Bond Earnings:	________.____
2w – Principal on Fixed Income instruments:	________.____
Total Haram Earnings:	________.____

Worksheet #3: Expenses and Liabilities

Please fill in

4a – Monthly Living Expenses:	
Monthly Mortgage or Rental Payment	(_______.___)
Medical Expenses	(_______.___)
Groceries, Energy, Telecom	(_______.___)
Transportation, Petrol, upkeep	(_______.___)
Miscellaneous Living Expenses	(_______.___)
Total Monthly Living Expenses:	(_______.___)
4b – Periodic Insurance Payments:	
Home /Renter's Insurance	(_______.___)
Auto Insurance	(_______.___)
Medical Insurance	(_______.___)
Total Insurance Payments for the period:	(_______.___)

4g – Debts you owe to others:	(______.___)
	(______.___)
	(______.___)
Total	(______.___)

Expenses and Liabilities Totals

4a – Monthly Living Expenses:	(________.____)
4b – Insurance Payments:	(________.____)
4c – Property Tax Payments:	(________.____)
4d – Delinquent Tax Payments:	(________.____)
4e – Miscellaneous Fines:	(________.____)
4g – Debts you owe to others:	(________.____)
Total Expenses and Liabilities:	(________.____)

Worksheet: Find the Minimum Liable Amount (Niṣāb)

Please fill in the price per gram of silver

X – Today's Price for 1 gram of silver	______.____
Y – Multiply X by 595 grams:	______.____
Z- the cash value of the MLA (Niṣāb) of silver is:	______.____

The MLA (Niṣāb) this year is [insert line Z here]:	__________
Earliest date I have more than this amount is:	___/___/____
One year from this date is:	___/___/____
Was my savings greater than my MLA for the entirety of this period? Circle one:	Yes / No

Worksheet #4: Calculating your Zakat

A - Total Income and Earnings (from pg. 83):	________.____
B - Total Haram Earnings (from pg. 95)	(_______.___)
C - Permissible Wealth before deductions: [A minus B]	________.____
D - Total expenses and liabilities (from pg. 100):	(_______.___)
E – Total Wealth Liable for Zakat [C minus D]	________.____
F – Minimum Liable Amount (Niṣāb) as of ______ (date)	________.____
Is line E above greater than the amount in F?	**YES/NO**
Has line E been greater than line F for a year?	**YES/NO**
If you answered YES above, then multiply line E by 2.5%[33]. This is the total amount of Zakat you owe for this year.	________.____

---

[33] - Many people use a date in the Islamic Calendar to calculate their Zakat, like Ramadan or Hajj. If you are using a date on the Gregorian calendar, then you need to multiply by 2.578 to make up for the additional 11 days difference between the two calendar years.

Name 3 charities that you will give to, based on what you've read:

1)

2)

3)

Name 3 individuals that you will give to, based on what you've read:

1)

2)

3)

تم والحمد لله رب العالمين

Made in the USA
Columbia, SC
07 September 2024